Dry Rot and Daffodils

Behind the scenes in a National Trust house

MARY MACKIE

ORION

An Orion paperback

First published in Great Britain in 1994
by Victor Gollancz
This paperback edition published in 1995
by Victor Gollancz

Fourth Impression 2003

Reissued in 2001
by Orion Books Ltd,
Orion House, 5 Upper St Martin's Lane,
London WC2H 9EA

A CIP catalogue record for this book is available
from the British Library.

ISBN 0 75283 409 6

Printed and bound in Great Britain by
Clays Ltd, St Ives plc

Introduction

Along a narrow, tree-shaded driveway, evening sunlight glowed like flame on gold and orange azaleas. Rhododendron bushes hung heavy with bloom, from deepest purple through scarlet and pink to purest white, and woodland walks opened temptingly on either hand, leading to more flower-laden glades dappled with warm golden light. As the car topped a rise, the woods opened ahead of us to display undulating parkland and a glimpse of blue sea in a gap between the hills. In the valley a magnificent old house spread elegant walls and chimneys against a backdrop of trees that enclosed it like a shawl, guarding it from northeast winds. Well-tended gardens surrounded it, and a small lake reflected the cloud-drifted sky of a perfect summer evening . . .

The man beside me let out a sigh of utter contentment. 'All this, and getting paid for it, too.'

I had to smile. That was what *we* had thought, three years before.

My companion was new to the stately home business, having arrived only a day or two earlier to join us on the staff at Felbrigg Hall, in north Norfolk, and I was taking him to a private viewing of nearby Sheringham Hall, which the National Trust had recently acquired. Sheringham Hall is too small to be regularly open to the public, though its lovely park is there for all to see year-round. But on this occasion, the house being empty of tenants, we and other staff members were being given the chance to look round the Hall itself.

My husband, Chris, could not accompany us. Someone had to remain behind to babysit our own property, and since at Felbrigg only two people are employed as permanent house staff,

5

one or other of them has to be there, twenty-four hours a day, three hundred and sixty-five days a year.

But I understood our new colleague's euphoria; sometimes, even after three years, I still felt the same way.

Until Edwardian times and the approach of the Great War, an army of servants kept a great house in order for the benefit of one family and its guests. Nearly a century on, a handful of people provide much the same service for the benefit of hundreds of thousands of summer visitors, in mansions which now belong to the nation. For the staff of a stately home, this means an eventful life, full of frustrations, endless worries, a lot of laughter, maddening interruptions, unexpected delights, suddenly erupting problems, and just a few moments of pure magic. One day you're clearing up excrement, or crawling through a void between floors, covered from scalp to sole in cobwebs and dead flies, finding dried mice and bats in inaccessible areas, and the next you're being introduced to Extremely Important Persons such as . . . well, read on and you'll find out who our own very special visitor turned out to be.

My earlier book *Cobwebs and Cream Teas* told the story of our first year as novices in the game, after my husband was appointed as houseman at Felbrigg Hall. The book brought a warm response from all over this country and from abroad, with many requests for me to give talks about life behind the scenes with the National Trust, and a host of enquiries as to when I was going to write more on the subject. To all those who took the trouble to let me know they had enjoyed the first book, thank you. This new book, *Dry Rot and Daffodils* has been written for you. It tells of some of our adventures after Chris was promoted to the post of administrator – that is, in full charge of the property and able to implement some of his own ideas for it, while still inevitably being embroiled in the day-to-day problems of cleaning, workmen and visitors.

Though the stories here tell of our own personal experience, from the many letters and calls I've had from staff at other properties I know that what happened to us is mirrored at stately homes all over the country, not only those belonging to national organizations but those in private ownership, too. To their keepers go my best wishes and tons of fellow feeling. Long may you continue to guard our nation's heritage.

Mary Mackie
Heacham, Norfolk
1994

1

Daffy-down dillies and other signs of spring

The last squire of Felbrigg observed that, 'The spring is always cold and late on the Norfolk coast.' True as this may be in certain chilly years, the camellias in the Orangery start to bud in January, snowdrops floor the February woods, and by the time the Hall opens to the public, around Easter, we confidently expect our usual show of daffodils to be in flower. Each spring they spread their dancing yellow across the pasture which fronts the old house, ready to welcome the first visitors of the season.

As every gardener knows, though, daffodils growing in grass demand special care: faded flowers should be allowed to die back naturally, thus returning their nourishment to the bulbs. Since this means leaving the grass to grow untrimmed until the daffodil leaves wither, you may imagine the height our grass can reach before our park-keepers decide it's time to cut the whole area, daffodils and all.

Thus, for several weeks in spring and early summer, Felbrigg wears a shaggy green apron embroidered with wild flowers. Through this lush growth, a tarmac path leads visitors to the iron railing and the gate which guards the shingled, semi-circular front courtyard.

While the knee-high pasture lasts, it is a miniature nature reserve all of its own. Our gardeners don't use chemical weed-killers, so the grass is gay with ragwort and ox-eye, buttercups and clover, sprinkled with pretty moths and butterflies. If you lie prone on it, you'll see a whole hidden world, a jungle crawling with spiders, ants and beetles of extraordinary beauty. But most of our human visitors skirt round it, using the defined pathway, so these oases of wildness lie undisturbed, a refuge for voles and mice.

A load of hay and three partridge eggs

One year, the deep pasture proved too great a temptation to a pair of red-legged French partridges. They built their nest in a patch bounded on two sides by the front railings of the Hall and on a third by the main front path, which is mostly used by pedestrians although it does see its share of cars driven by disabled drivers, who are allowed to park in the gravel courtyard. The birds apparently scorned the dangers from such vehicles, or from two-legged giants and their dogs, coming and going only a few yards from their retreat, not to mention several resident cats which prowled the park by night. Down in their cosy hollow the partridge parents could not be seen, so they felt safe. The female laid her eggs and began to brood.

Once we had noticed the nest from a window of our flat above, we warned everyone not to disturb the spot. Any child seen ploughing merrily through the long grass was inveigled away, perhaps with a bribe of being allowed a glimpse of the hen sitting, though we didn't like to go too close for fear of frightening her away. *EastEnders* had nothing on this natural soap opera as we anxiously awaited developments.

By peering with binoculars from our flat, at a moment when the hen was occupied elsewhere, we saw three eggs, a delicate bluey-green with fawn speckles. We knew they were still alive because the hen was never away for long; she kept returning to settle her feathers and keep her brood warm, while we foolish humans watched for signs of hatching, enthralled by the drama – like surrogate grandparents.

Now, I have to tell you that the National Trust tries not to waste any of its resources. That being so, when the daffodils are done, the long Felbrigg grass is subjected to the attentions of a haybaler. If you arrive at the right moment, you may see a couple of huge hayrolls, neatly wrapped in polythene, adorning the frontage of the Hall while waiting to be speared and borne

The partridges built their nest in a patch bounded
on two sides by the front railings and on a third
by the main front path . . .

away on the prongs of a tractor. Felbrigg looks like an old lady who has stuffed a couple of curlers in her fringe, anxiously anticipating a special outing.

In the year of the partridge, we were the ones who waited anxiously. Passing time made the grass grow taller; wild flowers flourished, moths lifted and fell like thistledown, and the daffodil leaves withered. All too soon the haybaler, with its churning cutters and binders, hove into sight, ready to give the pasture its first haircut of the year.

'Can you be a bit careful, please?' Chris asked the driver. 'There's a nesting partridge in the grass. Look, I'll show you where . . . Don't disturb her. The eggs are about to hatch. If you frighten her away now she'll never come back and the chicks will die.'

They went to view the spot, speaking in whispers and treading tippy-toe through yard-high jungle until the baler driver could see exactly where the speckled bird huddled over her vulnerable family. He, too, was eager to be protective. Yes, he understood; he'd give her a wide berth, even though it meant losing a bit of hay. He could always come back and cut it later, or our gardeners would include it in their regular mowing.

Fine. Happy that our small neighbour would remain undisturbed, we returned to our tasks in the Hall, while outside the tractor rumbled and churned, back and forth, round and round.

Trouble was, his idea of a 'wide berth' was different from ours – and the partridge's. He left a neat ring of long grass circling the nest, all of two feet wide! He meant well, I suppose, and it was his job to get as much hay as he could, but when he and his great noisy machine had gone the nest was empty, the eggs cold and deserted. The partridge hen did not come back.

In the great world plan, this tragedy was trivial, I know. With all the predators around, the chicks might well have perished before they could fly, prey to an owl, or a cat, or maybe a fox or a badger. Even so, we were sorry for them. After all, we were in the business of caring, for the environment and for our heritage, conserving and preserving for future generations. A load of hay and three partridge eggs . . . One of the more minor dramas of life at Felbrigg Hall.

A *flight of fancy*

To gain some idea of where we are and what Felbrigg is like, imagine being a seagull soaring in from the North Sea towards the top of East Anglia's pregnant bulge, thirty miles or so east of the Wash. You might see the crab and lobster boats out, hauling up their baskets from the buoys that bob across the water. High tide sends great breakers pounding at the foot of sandstone cliffs, across pebble beaches which, in summer, are thick with playing children and browning bodies. From the pretty fishing-town of Sheringham, the line of the steam railway curves off into the hills, heading towards Holt, skirting Sheringham Park and crossing the wild, gorse-covered heath at Kelling. Further east, the pier at Cromer juts into the sea, with the Gothic turrets of the Hotel de Paris standing on the cliff above it. The huge church tower soars nearby, and away to the left the lighthouse on its prominence shows white among the new houses of a holiday hamlet. The towns and villages along the coast are rich with the history of the sea – families of fishermen, bold lifeboatmen and daring smugglers.

Many miles of the coast are owned by the National Trust, the abode of wild creatures, birds and rare plants. But here and there a caravan site obtrudes its practical ugliness. Behind them, see the rolling fields and gently swelling hills of the hinterland.

This is north Norfolk, a glorious land of unspoiled villages hidden among wooded hollows. Many trees grow here, remnants of ancient woodland and some more recently planted by skilled landscapers with the vision to foresee how one day they would blend and form a feast for the eyes. In spring one can only wonder at the amazing variety of greens that nature flaunts; in summer the woods provide welcome shade; in autumn they burgeon with a palette of jewel colours, ruby and amber, tiger eye and jade . . .

On the outskirts of Cromer, the great swathe of Felbrigg woods begins, planted to protect the mansion from the worst chill of the winds that come straight from the Arctic. There's a lane known as the Lion's Mouth, some say because the trees that grow there look like jagged teeth, stretching over to enclose walkers and motorists; others say the name arose because of the redness of the leaves that lie under the trees in autumn. Whatever the real answer, at any season it's a lovely place, right on the edge of the woods, haunted by rabbits, jays and foxes. If you're lucky, you might glimpse a deer.

Fly on, over the woods where two rides meet to form the 'Victory V' which, it is said, helped to guide wartime bombers home. At the apex of the V there's a bench, placed by the last squire to commemorate his younger brother, who was killed in Crete in that same war. In spring the woods are white with snowdrops, yellow with primroses and daffodils, later misty with bluebells, then rich and juicy with blackberries. Deep among the trees lies an old icehouse, where once a pistol was found. It belonged to the last squire's mother. How did it get there? No one knows, but my novelist's imagination boggles.

Ah, now, see the dark American pines of the formal garden, the redwoods, the oaks, the great gnarled sweet chestnuts – the older they are, the more twisted they grow – and off to the left the walled garden, where vegetables and fruit flourish along with a wondrous collection of hawthorn, where glasshouses boast crops of grapes, limes and grapefruit, while an armless merboy presides over a pool where waterlilies spread dark leaves under huge, stunning flowers, both delicate pink and bright yellow.

But now, at last, here's the house below us, a great mass of wings and courtyards, a confusion of roofs and twisted barley-sugar chimneys. Its earliest above-ground part dates from 1620, but one of the cellars is even older. Various owners have added to it over the years and so it has grown, and gathered character. See where the dormer windows of the attics peer out across the lead-floored parapet, where you can walk high above the world, behind words of stone written across three bays: GLORIA – DEO IN – EXCELSIS. Not everyone realizes the inscription is a Latin text, declaring 'Glory to God in the highest'. Visitors have been known to approach the front door wondering about the identity of the lady whose memory is enshrined on the parapet: 'You know – the lady called Gloria.'

Soar on, over the house, across the open expanse of the park, dotted with oak and chestnut and even the odd elm still, despite the depredations of Dutch elm disease, and despite the great hurricane of '87. Can you see the church in its hollow, all alone now the village has moved away from it? And here's the lake below us, and more woods beyond, a rolling, gently fertile countryside of farms, with secret villages betrayed by round church towers built of flint. Far in the distance, twenty-five miles as the crow flies, on a clear day you can see the greatest spire of the county, reaching skywards on the cathedral at Norwich.

Many birds swoop about Felbrigg's Jacobean bays and Victorian castellations, passing the heraldic beasts which guard our parapets, perching on chimneys which are artworks of brick, and roofs whose slopes are lovingly clothed in Collyweston slates and whose hollows are lined with lead. Wagtail, martin and swallow, pigeon, sparrow and blackbird, all find their place about the eaves in due season, while Egyptian and other geese, ducks, hawks and honey buzzards haunt the park and lake. All of them delight us, as do the woodpeckers hammering in the woods, and the white doves which sail in phalanx from their cote in the walled garden to ornament the lawns as they preen their pristine feathers.

Once we even gave rest and shelter to a pelican, an amazing sight sailing unconcernedly across the lake, being given a wide berth by the resident swans, ducks, geese and moorhen. For days we watched him, calling all the nearby zoos and sanctuaries to see if they had lost such a bird. None of them had. Then one day the visitor was gone, leaving us to speculate as to where it came from. Can it really have been a wild pelican, flown all the way from Africa to rest among us exhausted on its way to . . .where?

Other, more common, creatures live around us, too: a breeding herd of cows in the lakeside meadows, joined by sheep now that a new farmer tenants the Home Farm; two donkeys in a paddock behind the Hall; a dog or two, and several cats, with the tenants; a scurry of mice now and then, voles, shrews, spiders, wasps, and, of course, the friendly toads whose abode is beneath our gratings. Not to mention the occasional rat.

Being close to Blickling Hall, which is regarded as the flagship of the National Trust, Felbrigg has at times tended to be a little overshadowed. Blickling, only eleven miles away, is larger; its rooms are more stately, its gardens more formal, and it has been in the care of the National Trust much longer. An earlier house on the same site has associations with Anne Boleyn, fated queen of Henry VIII, though no evidence has been found that she was ever there in person. And since the present house was rebuilt a century after her time, it is certainly *not* true, as an American visitor to Felbrigg was heard to be informing his companion, that 'Henry the Eighth built Blickling Hall for Anne Boleyn.' It's extraordinary how these misunderstandings persist.

But if Blickling has grandeur, Felbrigg is cosier – not so much a stately home as a country gentleman's residence. Many of our regular visitors prefer its more intimate atmosphere. They all say they can imagine people living there, inhabiting those rooms, sitting by those fireplaces on winter evenings and enjoying the paintings, the porcelain, the furniture, and the décor that ranges from eighteenth-century elegance to heavily ornate Victoriana.

The house faces south, its main state rooms being in the west wing with the utility areas to the east. Behind it, a grass courtyard was once a cobbled area, surrounded by laundry rooms, places for hanging game and other outhouses which are now turned into modern homes for a few tenants and staff. Further to the east is the castellated brick stable block, the last part of the house to be built, in Victorian times. It houses the new restaurant and shop.

High hopes

When we began our life at Felbrigg we knew that Robert, the administrator, was nearing retiring age. Naturally we hoped that Chris would have a chance for promotion when the time came, after three years to prove his worth as houseman. He was fairly sure he could do the job, and I, naturally, was convinced of it; but we knew that competition would be fierce and a more suitable candidate might appear. We could not take anything for granted.

However, early in the year when Robert's retirement was

pending, Chris and I were invited to attend a weekend staff conference at which Chris was the only houseman present, the rest being administrators and their wives. We took this as perhaps a hopeful sign that, even if he didn't get the job at Felbrigg, he might be considered suitable to take charge of another property. Meantime, whatever the portents, we determined to enjoy the few days at Madingley Hall, near Cambridge.

Madingley was the house where Prince 'Bertie' of Wales (later Edward VII) stayed when he was a student at Cambridge University; it is now used as a venue for conferences and study groups. In attendance over a long weekend packed with lectures and other activities were staff from all over south-east England, affording a rare chance to get together and swap tales of our experiences, discovering that we shared many similar joys, woes, gripes and funny stories. We also had the chance to listen to personnel from various regions: historic buildings representatives, who advise on conservation; land agents, who manage the farms and parks; foresters, who look after the woods; public relations experts; buildings managers and, inevitably, accountants. We also met some of the head office staff, including the Director General, Angus Stirling, who spoke about his vision of broadening the appeal of the Trust, changing its image so that a wider range of people would find it more accessible. It was in response to this talk that I finally got down to writing *Cobwebs and Cream Teas*, not as an erudite piece of literature about the Trust – other people have done that far better than I could – but as a light-hearted read about our life 'behind the scenes'.

Madingley was an unforgettable experience. A particular privilege was a visit to the Hamilton Kerr Institute in Cambridge, where we saw being restored vast paintings from Belton House and from Hampton Court (water-damaged after the 1986 fire). There was also a Van Dyck portrait which, having been summarily cut from its frame by thieves, was recovered thanks to BBC television's *Crimewatch UK* and was now being repaired with painstaking care, every fibre being reattached. Apart from being riveted by the secrets we were shown, I took notes for a possible future murder mystery – my imagination never stops work.

In lectures during the weekend we were exhorted to think of

new ways to popularize the Trust, which is still seen in some circles as being stuffy and reactionary; we were told we must look to the future, think of ourselves more as part of the tourist industry, find ways of attracting more visitors while never losing sight of our primary objective, which is to preserve places of beauty in perpetuity for the nation. The speakers all stressed the importance and value of property administrators. 'You are in the front line, the visible face of the Trust. On you rests an enormous responsibility.'

Heady stuff.

What with visits to properties, study projects, talks and discussions, the weekend at Madingley proved stimulating. Replete with good food and mellowed by evening sessions in the bar with like minds, some of whom became good friends, we all went home thoroughly inspired and optimistic.

A *new broom*

As the time for Robert's retirement approached, the post was widely advertised and Chris submitted his application along with the rest. We learned later that several hundred hopefuls had sent in their forms and CVs – jobs with the Trust are always keenly sought. However, Chris was short-listed and attended an interview with the regional director and the chairman of the regional committee. There followed an agonizing wait (only overnight, though it seemed like days) until we heard that Chris had been appointed by unanimous decision. So we could stay at Felbrigg, move into the larger flat in the main part of the Hall, and Chris would take on responsibility for the day-to-day running of the property, with the help of a new houseman yet to be appointed.

It was an exciting moment. Chris had long been developing plans and schemes to help put Felbrigg more clearly on the map and our weekend at Madingley had indicated that such innovations would be welcomed. Now was his chance to see if his ideas would work.

The news that he had won the job met with a varied reaction, mostly warm and congratulatory, though some of the old guard

were a little surprised. His sense of humour isn't always appreci-
ated by those staid souls who believe that looking after a stately
home should be a serious business.

Whatever their immediate feelings, however, the staff and
volunteers knew that there would be a strong hand at the helm.
They might not always agree with him, but they understood
that Chris cared deeply about Felbrigg; he had his own vision
of what it might become and he fought for it, and for his staff.
Inevitably this meant occasional clashes – even with head office
when some general decree struck him as unsuitable for Felbrigg
– but he had powerful allies among like-minded individuals with
a strong interest in Felbrigg, including some of our guides and
regular visitors. It made for lively times.

We began with high hopes and aspirations, and I for one was
riding on a wave of euphoria. 'I always knew you'd be lady of
the manor some day,' my darling dad laughed, delighted for us.
Perhaps I did feel a touch of hubris (let's be honest, I had a *lot*
of hubris!) but that mostly got knocked out of me as reality
returned to remind me that in the stately home business the
glamour is always balanced by grime and grind. Still, I never
lost the thrill of driving down that long oak-tunnelled driveway,
knowing I was going home while others could spend only a day
there.

For Chris, though, doing a good job was the main thing. That
has been his main motivation for as long as I've known him:
whatever work he is doing comes first. He enjoyed his new
role, but he never succumbed to the fantasy of playing squire,
however briefly. Our elder son, Andrew, away at Nottingham
University studying for a Ph.D., considered that it was our life,
nothing to do with him. I don't think he ever felt that Felbrigg
was 'home' – he mourned the bungalow we had been obliged
to sell. It was left to our younger son to acquire the green wellies,
the waxed jacket and the flat tweed cap. Kevin, a nurse then
based in Norwich, handy for visits, loved to bring friends over
for a meal, to go fishing in the lake or take someone's dog for
a walk in the woods, with a long stick to beat back brambles.
He often dropped in with a few of his medical friends.

In fact, we suddenly became very popular with a lot of old

friends and acquaintances who would pop over for a meal, or spend a night or two, or simply turn up unexpectedly in the middle of a busy day and be surprised to find we hadn't time to stand and chat for hours. Many people seem to think that working for the National Trust is a pleasant haze of lazy days amid elegant surroundings.

Chris's new job meant he was in even more need of a willing wife to act as hostess, backstop and general voluntary assistant, helping out whenever an extra pair of hands was needed at short notice. This worked out as a daily call at times, with an unforgettable few months when I was official houseman. But for more of that read on ...

Moving house – just next door

The houseman's flat lies over the Old Kitchen, looking on to the grass courtyard and the rear of the house. The administrator's apartment is at the front, partly in the main house, spacious accommodation with rooms on two or three floors. It has a staircase whose nine flights run right from the cellars to the attics (with doors to close off draughtier areas, I'm pleased to report). It took me a long while, flying up and down about my household chores, or dashing to answer phones, to get the hang of which floor I was on. I often caught myself rushing into the bedroom, mistaking it for the kitchen two flights below, or dashing down the next two flights and finding myself at our private front door when I was actually heading for the loo.

With the houseman's flat being connected by a door to one of the administrator's bedrooms (we called it the Brown Room because of its carpet), we decided that we could manage to move ourselves, with help from Kevin, who offered to come over for a few days. There was no hurry, which was just as well since with no houseman and the season in full swing we were both occupied by the demands of the Hall. I had to help if Chris wasn't to run himself into the ground, but since it was a temporary imposition I smiled and looked pleasant about it as, in between other jobs, we began our house-removal. For a while we were living partly in both flats, and naturally, thanks to

Murphy's law, whatever we suddenly had need of was miles away in other regions of the sprawling house.

The main problem in moving was that the door from the Brown Room into the main flat was only two-thirds the width of a normal door, and at the bottom of six awkward steps. However, most of our furniture would go through, with care and a little dismantling; a larger wardrobe we could conveniently leave in the Brown Room; the only real problem was our three-piece suite, one chair and two solidly made beech settees, none of which would go through that narrow door. The only answer was to take them right through the old flat, down a long flight of stairs and out into a hallway, through the Old Kitchen, along a couple of corridors to the ground-floor door of our new flat, then up two flights of stairs with a difficult turn in them and down another passageway to what was to be our main living/dining room. Somehow, Chris and Kevin managed it with me anxiously looking on and lending what help I could. Time, thankfully, has veiled the worst of the language.

The kitchen in the administrator's flat was antiquated – for one thing, the only means of heating water to the sink was a tiny boiler that could warm about two pints at a time. I often wonder how Robert and Eve, our predecessors, ever managed. However, our friends at regional office had agreed that the room should be modernized and workmen came and stripped it to barest essentials, taking out the ancient sink and cupboards, leaving only a useful bank of wall-to-ceiling cupboards which had once held the house's linen. Oh – and our cooker was, thank goodness, left connected, though it sat isolated in the middle of bare floorboards in an otherwise empty room.

I was delighted to be given the chance to choose colours for the new cupboards and flooring, and to decide what sort of sink I would like, but given the age of the room, and its different functions through different incarnations, the modernizing was not straightforward. For instance, the new sink had to be situated across an old fireplace *without making any permanent changes to that fireplace*. We lived in chaos for three or four weeks, ending up with a mantelpiece over our drainer, which if nothing else made a talking-point. But then all our rooms had some sort of oddity about them, much more interesting than living in a modern house, and our visitors loved to be shown round the nooks and crannies.

As you may imagine, preparing meals during the kitchen remodelling was a problem. Breakfast and a snack lunch we managed, but a hot evening meal was more difficult with everything to be brought from different rooms, no surfaces to work on and no sink. However, upstairs next to the echoing bathroom with its sixteen-foot ceiling, there remained an equally tall, narrow slop room (once used by housemaids to clean out chamberpots and other utensils), which still had its great stone sink. I used that for vegetable preparation and washing up.

A thin partition wall, built right across an enormously tall window, separates the slop room from a long, thin, very tall sliver of a room with a magnificent loo at the end of it, its seat and tank cover made of polished mahogany. This room always caused gales of laughter whenever some new guest saw it. But it had a lovely view over the rear garden. You could sit happily on the mahogany for hours watching the visitors stroll among the shrubberies and lawns.

When our friends among the guides realized the problems we were having with the kitchen, they rallied round to help. One friend seemed to come nearly every day with something wrapped in a cloth and we would find on our stairs a delicious casserole, or a pie, which could easily be heated in our oven and give us a well-balanced meal. Others brought apples by the load, or trout from a nearby lake, or home-made wine to cheer us. Such kindness made our frantic lives much easier.

A good idea, but . . .

Chris had thought that a regular newsletter would be a good way of passing on messages and reminding people of dates, generally trying to build up a team feeling so that everyone felt a part of what was going on at Felbrigg. Some of the guides handed in snippets of news and funny stories, all of which were included. Collating the information and then typing it up on my word processor took hours, not that I minded – I have always loved working with words. At the time, the only secretarial help Chris had was from Jill, who came in on a Sunday afternoon and whose few paid hours were always filled with official work. The rest of the paperwork he had to do himself, or rope in someone who happened to be handy. Guess who?

One evening after the Hall was closed, when we had completed the usual lockdown security routine and Chris had dealt with the paperwork and reconciling of cash that had to be done every evening, we quickly enjoyed the casserole Sallie had left and then returned to the office to photocopy the newsletter and address about eighty envelopes. Everyone was to get a copy of our first newsletter – shop and restaurant managers and their staff, gardeners and woodsmen, cleaners, recruiters, nearby tenants and, not least, our huge team of volunteer guides.

Only as we were sealing the last few envelopes did I notice that a vital date was wrong. All the envelopes had to be opened again, the mistake corrected, and the envelopes taped down . . . It was long after midnight before we finished.

Everyone seemed to like the newsletter. They all asked why we didn't do it more often. Perhaps now they'll understand why only three or four editions ever saw the light. There just weren't enough hours in the day.

A houseman I would be . . . maybe

When the houseman's post was advertised, more applications flooded in. At the interviews I acted as receptionist and also showed the candidate couples round the flat which we had vacated. Some of them were as round-eyed with amazement as we had been three years before; others were confident – 'I could do this job with my eyes shut,' said one; yet others seemed to imagine there would be lots of free time during the evenings and in the winter when they might pursue personal interests (deluded souls!). Some of the wives, however, had doubts: 'It's a bit isolated, isn't it? Three miles to the nearest shop and I don't drive. Is it haunted? The flat's a bit strange . . . Where do you hang your washing out?' (The answer is that you don't, unless you can beg room on a tenant's line and have the time and energy to walk the long distance between. During most of the time we spent in the houseman's flat, our washing had hung over an airer in the bathroom. In the new flat, it hung more conveniently in that handy slop room.)

The new appointee moved to Felbrigg in June, but stayed with us only six months and left just before we were due to take our annual break the following January. Knowing that Chris would be without a proper assistant again until the job could be re-advertised and a new set of interviews arranged – several weeks, at the least – we snatched a last-minute package break to Malta before embarking on another hectic session of winter work. In our absence, our friends George and Ruth Blake moved in and ran the Hall. George had been custodian at another property but was now retired, acting as peripatetic stand-in at houses around the country in cases of illness or other emergency. Fortu-nately he lived nearby and sometimes came as a room warden when we were short-handed, so we knew we were leaving Fel-brigg in safe hands.

After our return from a marvellous holiday in the sun, Chris settled down to undertake the bulk of the work of both adminis-trator and houseman, with unofficial help from me. George Blake continued to stand in on Fridays to allow us a few hours off each week, for which we were grateful.

The Hall was full of the usual winter teams of workmen, mending, painting, tearing down and building up, and, of course, the cleaning was going ahead. Everything had to be co-ordinated, a watchful eye kept on safety and security, and the office and housekeeping continued; Chris had thought he was done with climbing scaffolding to get at plaster ceilings with the fine-tube vacuum head he had invented, but he found himself back at those heady heights, and when it came to the chandeliers we all lent a hand, and then there was the sewage overflow, and the problems with the lake, and . . .

It was early March by the time the next set of prospective housemen was being interviewed. Once again I showed short-listed hopefuls round the flat, trying to point out the downside of the life as well as the obvious attractions. We didn't want our next helper to come with all his illusions intact; he had to know it was a hard, dirty, demanding job, full-time in the real sense of the word – while you're on site, you're on duty, never mind that you might be entertaining guests when an emergency crops up, or lying in your sick bed, or having a bath, or a nervous breakdown.

Chris and the others on the interview panel all agreed that a man named Eddie was the best choice for the job. Unfortunately, Eddie was just finishing a career from which he couldn't be released until the end of June. What was to happen in the meantime? Chris couldn't be expected to carry on alone for nearly four more months without proper help. We chewed over possibilities for a while, reaching no conclusion. Anyway, it was nothing to do with me; I left them to it and went to get on with my own neglected work.

A couple of days later, when George Blake arrived to deputize while we had our Friday out and about, I walked into our kitchen and caught the tail-end of a conversation, with George saying something about, '. . . if Mary doesn't mind.'

'If Mary doesn't mind what?' I enquired.

There was a loud silence, a meeting of glances between the two men. 'Oh, sorry,' George muttered. 'Haven't you told her?'

It transpired that I had been 'chosen', by common consent between Chris and our land agent, Simon, to be acting houseman until Eddie could join us – four months of opening up and closing down the big house, shepherding workmen, dealing with conservators, keeping a watch on visitors and staff, supervising cleaners, generally being around to do whatever came up. I should like to say that I leapt at the chance, but I fear I was less than chuffed. Unqualified, uninterviewed, unasked! My writing work had already been disrupted by all the upheaval; I had stood in on what I thought was a very temporary basis in an emergency; damn it, I didn't want the darned job! But I didn't have much choice. I knew what Chris would say if I refused – that he would do it himself. That was always his answer if I balked at heaving heavy carpets, or moving ten-ton bronzes, or handling vast pictures. So, naturally, being concerned for his well-being, I capitulated, however grit-toothed.

One slight consolation was that I was to be paid, though not the full houseman's salary — after all, went the reasoning, I wouldn't need to be paying rent since Chris was already doing that. Still, the offer was fair enough and did mollify me a little. A writer's income can be precarious; at least this would be regular money.

Once I had resigned myself to the inevitability of my fate for the next four months, things calmed down a little. Most days Chris obligingly did the early opening-up which is usually the houseman's task — he's an early bird and I'm an owl (eight in the morning is still the middle of the night as far as I'm concerned). Otherwise, we managed the work between us, with me sometimes in the office doing clerking jobs while he did heavier houseman-type work. It was not the first time we had worked as a team and with a bit of mutual understanding we soon found ourselves falling into a routine.

We laughed one day when the restaurant staff called Chris to help them because there was a dead mouse in one of the traps and none of the ladies wanted to touch it. However, since *I* was houseman, *I* went and disposed of it. Not a task I relished, I admit, but doing it gave me satisfaction — at least I didn't wimp out.

The post of houseman is being renamed as house steward now. This may help to avoid the kind of confusion that had arisen earlier when Chris broke his thumb in the heavy outer door leading to the ladies' lavatories. He was never quite sure how he had done it, except that he had left his thumb there a fraction too long and the door slammed on it. He took himself to hospital and an X-ray confirmed a fracture, which was strapped up in a 'spiker' plaster. The doctor who attended him asked what his job was and Chris, not thinking, said he was a houseman. He did wonder vaguely why the doctor then became very chatty and was talking about other casualty patients in an unusually open manner. It was when he said: 'I didn't realize you had patients up at Felbrigg Hall. What kind of a hospital is it?' that Chris had to explain that he was not the junior hospital doctor kind of houseman but a man who looked after a house. Abrupt end of confidential conversation!

Camellia-nappers

On a bright cold day one February, Chris and I happened to glance out of a window, across the view of winter-bare gardens, to see some people climbing up the ha-ha (the sunken wall that guards part of the garden). Mother and father, with three children between eight and fifteen, were scrambling up, and then kindly helping poor old granny up after them – she had a bit of trouble because of her stiff knees.

At that time of year the park and woods are open, as they are all year round, acres and acres for people to wander in freely, but the house and gardens are closed to the public, still resting before the onslaught of tramping feet and enquiring hands. That winter rest is necessary for the house and gardens to recover, for cleaning and renovation to be done to the building and its contents, while outside replanting and reseeding, tree-lopping, and other possibly dangerous activities take place in controlled conditions without risk to public well-being. However, there are always a few visitors who don't appreciate our reasons for denying them access at any time. Like this family. Just the latest of several who, through the winter, penetrate our defences.

For a few minutes we stood and watched them in sheer amazement. Having managed to scale the ha-ha, they vanished behind a bank of trees, heading deeper into the gardens. Chris set off to discover what they were doing – security was, after all, part of his job.

By the time he reached them – through the flat, via corridors and passageways to the garden entrance, and then across lawns and round shrubberies – the trespassers were in the Orangery, each one laden with an armful of red, white and pink-speckled camellias nestling amid dark glossy leaves. They had virtually stripped the lower branches, decimating the flowers on the eighty-year-old trees.

The father's explanation was that it was a lovely day and he and his family had come out for a drive. Finding themselves in Felbrigg Park, they had fancied a walk in our gardens, only to find themselves forced to climb in because all the gates were locked. What else did we expect people to do when every usual

'They were just growing free . . .'

access was shut up? As for the camellias . . . well, they didn't belong to anybody, did they? They were just growing free, there for the taking. Still, if Chris was going to be awkward, he could have his so-and-so flowers. And he threw down the camellias he was carrying, bidding his family do the same, leaving the flowers strewn on the gravel path. From my window far away I watched as the intruders returned with difficulty down the ha-ha, helping granny after them, knocking off lumps of the ancient wall as they went.

A saddened Chris gathered up the fallen blooms and brought them back to the flat, where we put them in water. But the lovely waxen petals soon went brown and died. They always do when they are removed from where they belong. If only they had been left on their branches, some of those fresh buds would have given delight for weeks, well into the open season, providing pleasure for hundreds of people.

The spice of life

The main cleaning has its own schedule, which runs through late autumn and winter. To begin with, in preparation for in-depth cleaning, in the first two weeks after the Hall has closed to the public all china, porcelain, glass, bronzes, boxes and knick-knacks are wrapped in acid-free paper and stored safely away. Furniture is protected by case-covers or dust sheets. Curtains are usually left *in situ*, but their ties are removed and the folds teased out so that the air can get into the folds. They are then vacuum cleaned, through a firm plastic mesh so that the fabric is not distorted or even, if fragile, sucked up the hose! Then, room by room, the china, porcelain and glass is washed in a special toxic-free detergent called Synperonic N, dried, and put back into store, while wooden furniture receives its annual coat of pure beeswax and linseed oil. Walls and paintings are brushed free of dust and cobwebs and, finally, the cleaners take their vacuum to the carpets – again using special care with old and valuable weaves.

The books in the library take up five or six weeks of the winter cleaning programme. Each section of books is carefully removed from its place before being examined for damage and the tops dusted with a dry shaving brush – which is also used to remove any obvious debris between covers and pages. The cleaners are our first line of defence against the ravages of beetle, bookworm or plain damp.

The houseman supervises the winter work and does high-level cleaning himself, by means of scaffolding from which he can reach intricate plaster ceilings and inaccessible corners. Readers of *Cobwebs and Cream Teas* may remember that when Chris was carrying out this cold and dusty task he discovered the tiny animals in the ceiling of the Cabinet. Housekeeping is a vast subject: from what started as a loose-leaf binder of preferred practices, the Trust has published its own manual of cleaning techniques, which makes fascinating reading.

The administrator, meanwhile, has charge of the office, which, as in every business, is bombarded with phone calls and letters on divers subjects. Another of his functions is the overall co-ordination of the different work going on in the house. Inevitably, workmen come in, mending shutters, perhaps, or fixing new security bars in attics and cellars, seeing to the score of jobs that seem to crop up weekly. Special meetings may take place in the Morning Room, which has to be prepared and warmed through – the houseman may be detailed to do that, if he has time; experts come to look at pictures; official photographers need access; people may be given permission to do research in the Library; the media want interviews, and all the time security has to be a priority. Chris's diary notes one period when for three solid days he had appointments every half-hour from nine in the morning until four in the afternoon, which didn't leave him much time for any last-minute callers who might need his attention. Very few days go as planned and extra complications seem to arise hourly. The administrator must be a man of many parts, and a bit of a juggler, able to think on his feet.

And, of course, there are the unexpected letters which arrive requesting pictures of certain things, or information that may take hours to get together and put on paper. We're always delighted to have someone show an interest in Felbrigg, but sometimes these requests have to wait their time in the queue.

National Trust properties do not have a large staff of experts waiting to answer queries, or take photographs, or do research. It is all down (mostly) to the administrator and his assistant.

Throughout the year, our own Trust experts and advisers also need attention when they arrive, by appointment usually, though sometimes they turn up without warning and may be dismayed if the administrator already has a full schedule and can't fit them in. For instance, the head housekeeper pays an annual visit; architects come to look at the fabric of the building; a young woman preparing the new guide book needs to look round; someone else is photographing everything in the house for the first proper inventory. Picture frames, security, heating, electrics, boilers, freezers, alarms, clocks, furniture, you name it, there is an expert who will at some time come along and need access to part of the house. Some of these visitors know the place well and can be left on their own; others have to be supervised. If three or four are here at the same time, the administrator and the houseman become split personalities!

Take a Tuesday in March, for example

When we closed in October it seemed that we had ample time to get everything done, but as the old year ends and the new one starts running away at frightening speed, life becomes increasingly hectic. Perhaps I could illustrate by detailing one particular day, a Tuesday in March.

The appointments diary looks fairly empty, with only three events expected: 11 a.m. a hygiene seminar in the Old Kitchen, for the restaurant staff; 1.30 p.m. room stewards gathering in the Morning Room to hear a talk given by Netta, one of our longest-serving volunteers; and later in the afternoon some pictures are due to be brought back and rehung, timed for 2.30 p.m. though the picture-hangers could arrive at any moment after lunch – it depends how long their journey takes. A nice easy day? Well, on paper, yes. The diary also notes an evening engagement for one of us to speak at a Women's Institute meeting, but that, thank goodness, was changed to another day. Just as well . . .

We start as usual by opening up the house in readiness for

the cleaners, who arrive at half past eight in the winter. At that stage of the year they are in the final throes of preparing the house for our first visitors of the season. The furniture is taken from under its dust covers and set in place, freshly dusted; it has been given its annual polish during the winter (more than that is unnecessary and clogs the wood's pores; only a thin layer of polish is needed as a protection, and to help the dust slide off easily). The porcelain comes out from its acid-free wrapping paper and is set out on sideboards and dressers. The glassware, too, sparkling in the light, returns to its show places, as do all the smaller items that make the house appear like a home – the pens in their tray on the desk; the letter-scale; the magazines on a side table; the breakfast trays beside the beds; the towels on their rails . . .

While our indispensable cleaners are busy at their work, I answer the back door and let in a set of workmen who need to be in our flat to fix shutters. After that they will want access to the cellars, where they are securing extra bars across the windows, and then they must be shown the window-frames which need attention in the stableyard.

In the afternoon, our volunteers will be gathering to hear a talk on some of the rare books we have in the Library. Usually these books remain closed all year, disturbed only once when the cleaners perform their annual miracle of dusting and checking every one of the thousands of volumes in the house. Neither room wardens nor visitors are allowed to open any of them; in everyday routine, only house staff ever handle them, and then with immense care. However, the Trust provides machinery by which scholars and researchers may be allowed to come and use the Library, with special permission from the Libraries Adviser at head office, and once in a while a team of conservators may come and spend a few weeks repairing the precious tomes.

Today, though, Chris has to get out some of the more interesting books for Netta's discourse that afternoon, so he and I, wearing white cotton gloves so that grease from our skin does no harm, get out what Netta has asked for and transport them, a few at a time, down to the safety of the Butler's Pantry. Considering the difficulties of finding the right books, the care that must be taken, the fact that some of them weigh a ton, and the distance between the Library and the Butler's Pantry, this all takes far longer than expected. In between whiles I keep a check on the workmen in our flat. Have they finished yet? When will they need to get into the cellar?

At the same time Joan, the restaurant manager, is in the kitchen baking cakes to go in the freezer, ready for the season. Joan is expecting her staff of waitresses, cooks and washers-up to arrive before long to attend the hygiene seminar for which she is also expecting the delivery of some equipment. But she will supervise these activities herself and has agreed to keep an eye on callers at the back door while we're busy elsewhere.

She reminds us that the striplights in the kitchen have not been cleaned yet (a houseman job), though the cleaners have washed down the walls and done everything else. So Chris gets out a stepladder (I'm not good at heights) and takes down the striplights; I clean them and he puts them back up while I hold the steps. He also cleans the extractor fans on the windows, and the electric fly-killer, the rehanging of which, on its chains, somehow takes all three of us.

Good, that's done. Joan rewards us with coffee.

The guides' meeting is to be held in the Morning Room, which is still laid out for the convenience of the sewing team who come in every Thursday (more about them later). Waiting until the cleaners have finished in the lobby, we reorganize the Morning Room with tables in a U-shape, with a horseshoe of forty-odd chairs set round them. Now we don cotton gloves once again and bring the books from the Butler's Pantry to arrange them ready for the talk.

While we're doing that, the workmen come to find us and Chris goes off to let them into the cellar and show them exactly where the new bars are to go. When the back doorbell rings I hurry to answer it, since by now the hygiene seminar is well under way. I notice fresh muddy tracks all down the stone floor of the Red Corridor, from the trolley which brought in equipment for the seminar. The corridor had recently been scrubbed at great expense of energy and it will now need doing again, but hey-ho . . .

The callers at the door are more workmen, planning to install a new safe in a day or two. They want to weigh up the problems involved. I show them the place where the safe has to go, and the foreman frowns, shaking his head, rubbing his chin. 'That's a two-day job, that,' he decides. 'See, we'll have to shore up them stairs for a start. Hm. Don't like the look of that a bit. Going to be a tricky old job, that.'

Immensely cheered to know that yet another 'simple' job is going to turn into a marathon, I let them out and go to find Chris, to help him erect our internal scaffolding in the Dining Room, where belong two of the pictures we hope will be brought back today. That done, we hurry to the flat to whip up a gourmet lunch of Heinz soup and bread which we just have time to gulp down before the first of our guides arrives for the meeting.

While Chris helps out in the Morning Room, doing most of the handling and displaying of the books while Netta talks about them, I take charge of the office, filing and typing letters, answering the phone and watching out for the picture-hangers. Since they're coming from Cambridge they might arrive at any time. When two thirty arrives, with the volunteers' cars still parked in the courtyard, I run down to see what's happening and find most of the guides still hovering over the books, fascinated by a glimpse of treasures some of them have never seen before. The meeting overruns by half an hour, though it's always a joy to chat with our friends. Their enthusiasm is infectious; we look forward to the boost of their regular company when Easter comes.

Eventually the last of them departs, by which time we have started to restack the chairs and set them in their usual place in the bay under a dust cover. Then, cotton-gloved again, we return the precious books to their various places in the Library.

Just as that job is completed, the picture-hangers' van pulls up to the door and we help to unload and bring inside three large, unframed oil paintings. They have been cleaned and restored and must now be returned to their frames.

'We'll work in the Morning Room,' the hangers decide.

More rearranging of tables ensues. I go up to the flat and make a large pot of tea for the men.

When I return, they report that one of the canvases has stretched during conservation work and is now too big to go in the frame. What is to be done?

Phone lines between us and regional office start to hum: we need the advice of the historic buildings representative, our expert on pictures. He's in a meeting, too busy to be disturbed, says his secretary. Perhaps she can help? Not in this case, Chris decides. Since the decision has to be made, he'll make it himself. The pictures must be rehung today. Two of them are fine, already back in their frames; it's that third, stretched one . . .

The joiner being still in the house, Chris fetches him and shows him the problem. Perhaps he can help? 'No problem,' he says. 'I can shave a bit off the inside of the frame. Easy.'

With a little bit of jiggling, a tiny wedge here and a sliver off there, the picture is reframed.

Now all that remains is the rehanging.

This, too, sounds simple, until you remember at what height these pictures hang. Their unwieldy size, their weight and the delicacy of those ornate gilt and gesso frames makes the job extra fraught. And don't even *think* about their value.

Our internal scaffolding is ready in the Dining-Room, providing a steady base as we support the pictures from beneath while the hangers secure them to their hooks on the walls. A sweat-making time later, with only the last picture to go, the top section of the huge scaffolding has to be dismantled and the rest manoeuvred, on its casters, through into the Great Hall, taking care not to knock against precious furniture or walls. Extra care is needed near the place where the carpet is rotting.

The empty spot on the wall here is above another portrait, which hangs over a big marble-topped table which prevents us from getting the scaffolding close enough. Will the table support the weight of two men? Gingerly, Chris tests it under his own weight, only to discover that even then he's not quite high enough to reach the picture-hooks. And, being Health and Safety Representative for the East Anglian region, he is not going to sanction any makeshift way of climbing up. The only answer is to move the table.

Even for four of us, the table is impossibly heavy, too close to the wall to get a good purchase, and we daren't risk tearing that delicate corner of the carpet. So Chris uses a method he has tried before with very heavy tables: he gets on hands and knees underneath it and lifts it with his back, just the few inches we need to get a proper hold on it. Then, with one at each corner, we somehow manage to carry it out of the way.

After that, the rest seems easy: we get the scaffolding in position and lock its casters before the experts climb up and we hand them the last huge portrait. We have to be careful not to catch the friable frame of the lower picture while we are sliding the new one up to where the hangers are waiting to take it. At last it's done, the scaffold can be taken away and the table replaced, again the last few inches crossed with Chris playing pack-elephant.

Visitors seeing that room on opening day will never dream of the involved work that has gone on here. It looks as if it has been sleeping all winter.

The picture-hangers finally left at about six o'clock, at which time Chris went to the office to catch up on paperwork and I, so the diary reminds me, went out to visit a friend in hospital. His wife was there too and, since she didn't drive, I gave her a lift home. By then too weary to think about cooking, I bought fish and chips on the way home. We ate about eight fifteen.

Next morning, the picture-hangers were in again, their task this time to check the chains and hooks of all pictures hanging in corridors, the ones in the main rooms having been done previously. We left them to get on with it while we turned to other chores, but mid-morning one of the cleaners came running in distress to inform us that the men were drilling holes in the walls of the staircase hall, sending dust everywhere. The cleaners had just completed polishing that area which, with its knobbly balusters, and the stairs, and the carpets, and the high-up busts, is a nightmare of dust-traps. It would all have to be done again, just when every moment was booked in the countdown to opening.

Mind you, as we gnashed our teeth in frustration we heard that things were even worse at Blickling Hall. There, every room was still in chaos – floors up, panelling off the walls, furniture all anyhow – owing to some belated electrical rewiring which had turned out more complicated than expected.

Meanwhile . . .

Meanwhile, back in the Chinese Bedroom, a dry rot fungus had just found a perfect spot to settle, in the secret dark between two walls, where a shuttered window had been bricked in. Before long, all unobserved and unsuspected by any human in the house, the dry rot had sprouted mycelia which were tentatively reaching out their probing, cobwebby little tendrils . . .

2

On the starting blocks . . .

Inevitably, there comes that Sunday in March when people look out of their window, see and smell the spring arriving, and want to shake off their winter wearies and get out in the sunshine. Where to go, though? Bit cold for the beach. Let's head for Felbrigg and take a walk. On such a day, Felbrigg's car-park can be almost as full as in the summer, with visitors and their dogs and children wandering about the lake and woods.

On just such a day, we were busy inside the Hall moving a heavy Queen Anne bureau, a lovely piece. Its burr walnut veneer had been faded by spending too many years in direct sunlight, but during the winter it had been in the care of Alan, our furniture restorer, and, thanks to his expertise, that lovely patterned wood was gleaming with a fresh golden patina. He had brought it back a couple of days before; now it had to be replaced in its proper setting.

Chris and I were in the front lobby, struggling to manoeuvre the bureau, when we saw a man peering in through a front window. He must have climbed over the front railing, where locked gates guard the approach court. When he saw us, he rapped on the glass and started shouting unintelligibly.

Sighing over yet another interruption, Chris got out his keys and went to open the front door.

'Can I help you?'

'Yes, you can. Aren't you open? *Why* aren't you open?'

'We open at the end of the month,' said Chris.

'What? Well, good heavens, man, what's a week or two matter? There are dozens of people around. Why can't you just

'Why can't you just open the doors
and let us all in?'

open the doors and let us all in? What difference would it make?'

It took some time to explain exactly what our problems were and why we couldn't just fling open the doors and let the world and his wife wander about when we had no staff on duty, no restaurant open, no shop . . . The man remained unconvinced. He appeared to think that a stately home must be fully staffed all year round.

What would we do without our volunteers?

The new roster for room wardens is completed by the administrator well before the season starts. He sends out forms on which our volunteers note the days they are willing to come. Some do three days a week, others one day per fortnight – however much they choose, or can fit in with other demands on their time. Each year, inevitably, some volunteers will drop out and new ones will join us; others want to change their days. All of this has to be juggled so that each room is covered on every open day. No doubt the finished roster will contain a few gaps, but helpers are always ready to step in to do extra shifts at short notice, and if we have a real problem Chris leaves a list on the Morning Room table, where the guides gather every day, and names appear as if by magic to fill the empty spaces.

The same is true of special events, when extra voluntary help is called for. Several times the list went out, expected to be completed gradually over the week, only for all spaces to be filled on the first day. This often led to complaints from those who didn't get a chance to volunteer for special duties! The whole team is full of enthusiasm and pride in Felbrigg, all for the pleasure of helping the National Trust; the travelling expenses they are paid often don't cover the cost of petrol, especially for those who live some distance away. But still they come. If it weren't for such stalwarts, the National Trust could not exist.

'Guides' Talks' are a feature of the early spring at Felbrigg, such as the one on books mentioned earlier. The more knowledgeable among our volunteers give lectures to their colleagues on aspects of Felbrigg or moments in history. One year they invited me to speak on the subject of Boudicca, who was once queen of the territory now known as Norfolk: I had just written a book about her so my research was up to date.

A talk by Chris became a regular event, eagerly anticipated because he could usually produce some surprise that even the longest-serving volunteer hadn't seen before. One of these talks he called 'Little Boxes'. Out from cupboards and strong rooms came some of the unsung small treasures of the house – a collection of silver boxes including vinaigrettes designed to hold sponges full of perfume, to protect the owner from nasty odours and, so it was thought by some, effective against disease; there are containers for pills, snuff, matches, and even tiny postage-stamp sized boxes meant to hold . . . you guessed it, stamps.

He included on the list the Armada chest he had discovered rusting away in the lock-up – a dank place with barred window and heavy metal door, once used (we believe) for holding poachers and similar miscreants overnight. The chest, found half-buried under a pile of old wood and other discarded oddments, has an intricate lock with seven bolts, and still bears its original painting of little men and boats; Chris brought it out, cleaned it up and stabilized it so it wouldn't deteriorate further. Another travelling chest, bound with wood, revealed inside four screws which passed through its base: the traveller would keep his valuables in it, and secure it to the floor of whatever house he was staying in. Once the lid was locked, it was proof against the opportunist thief, but one wonders what the owner of the house might have said on finding his floors chewed up in that cavalier fashion! Or might it, perhaps, have been fixed inside a closet?

At the back of a cupboard, Chris had found two antique chocolate boxes, cardboard models of a harp and a violin, fragile and superbly decorated. We tried to find out which firm made them but they don't seem to be English, so we guess perhaps Belgian. Or Swiss? Another question yet to be answered.

Lastly among the 'Little Boxes' was the smallest item on Felbrigg's inventory – a tiny Japanese box containing a tinier Japanese deity, some three-quarters of an inch high. Such things are too small to keep on display, except perhaps in a glass case, and since Felbrigg is presented as a home, not a museum, the dichotomy remains.

These talks gave Chris an idea which he hoped would allow him an opportunity to display a few more treasures to a few more people. He planned to bring this idea to fruition later in the year, under the title 'Beyond the Baize Door . . .'

Cutting comments

Even before the Hall itself opens, the park may be used for outside events. Occasionally the hunt meets there; a cycle race may come through, or a walking marathon; on more than one occasion our woods provided the venue for an orienteering event.

Going along to watch one of these last, in a downpour which had persisted all morning, I didn't envy the shivering competitors, up to their knees in thick, sticky mud and soaked to the skin, trying to find their way around the markers in the sodden woods.

I fell into conversation with a youngish chap who was eager to know all about Felbrigg. Being a keen National Trust member, he had visited a lot of properties, he said, but Felbrigg was new to him. 'Who have you got living in that cottage round by the wall?' he wanted to know. 'Whoever they are, they're not the sort the Trust ought to be letting places to.'

'What makes you say that?' I asked.

'Their curtains were still drawn when I came by – and they aren't even lined,' was the reply.

Unlined curtains, egad! Strange what some people think makes a suitable National Trust tenant.

That gentleman would probably have found plenty in common with the person who wrote to me after the local paper printed a piece on the publication of one of my novels – a mystery-romance. The letter said it was a crying shame that someone like me should be allowed to live at Felbrigg Hall and the last squire, a respected historian, would be turning in his grave in disgust if he knew. The writer omitted to sign a name, but since our address was given with not its correct post code but one appertaining to Felbrigg village, we guessed our correspondent lived nearby. It was nice to know we had friendly neighbours.

A stitch in time . . .

Among the many unexpected tasks at Felbrigg, now and then a needle becomes an essential tool. One year, while starting to set up the rooms ready for opening, Chris realized that the linen on display in the bedrooms – the towels which hang on the rails, the delicate tray cloths and runners with their lace edging – had not been laundered; so he washed and starched them himself, using that special concentrated detergent free of toxic chemicals. We whiled away a few idle evening hours repairing small tears and darning holes; then he carefully ironed all the pieces and put them back where their brightness helped to set off shining-clean rooms that were emerging from their winter sleep.

More stitches were needed, though not by us this time, thank goodness, when a damp patch appeared underneath a burr yew bureau in a corner of the Great Hall. An area of the carpet was rotting away and desperately needed emergency treatment. That carpet is of special interest: it bears in its corners the monogram of Victoria and Albert, and the date 1851; it was made for the Great Exhibition held in that year. Repairing it, even temporarily, was a job for experts from Blickling's famed fabric workshop, which looks after costumes and fabrics from all National Trust sources. Two of the ladies came over and spent a few days gently tacking a backing cloth to the rotting area, to consolidate it until more lasting repairs could be arranged.

The source of the damp was a mystery, the floor of the Great Hall being solid stone. One of the anomalies of Felbrigg is that there is no longer a cellar under this room; evidently one did exist, but no access to it remains. Holes which have been drilled through from other cellars around this area reveal only packed rubble. Chris wondered if the damp might be coming from outside. At the front of the house an angle between the Great Hall and the porch faces the prevailing wind and catches the worst of any driving rain. Often a puddle lies on the pea shingle of the front courtyard when everything else has dried up.

In due course, when workmen arrived to install a new drain from the downpipe, leading to a new soak-away, Chris asked them to connect it with that area of wetness in hope that it would serve to clear the problem. Time will tell if he was right or not – it takes years for rubble and stone to dry out properly – but it does seem a likely solution.

In the meantime, while the dampness in the carpet dried out, he laid some bituminized material under it to protect it, and the whole area was roped off so that no one could walk on the carpet.

The largest sewing job of all, however, concerned the making of a whole set of new case (dust) covers. Every winter, when the house was prepared for winter cleaning, the housekeeping team would cover all the furniture with huge, heavy dust sheets. In many rooms this meant storing the furniture in one area, so that it could all be covered at once under one or maybe two sheets, which made life awkward when some items had to be moved: everything would have to be uncovered again, perhaps to get at one chair or a certain mirror, and when that room came to be cleaned the furniture was always in the way. Nor was it good for some delicate pieces to have the weight of thick dust sheets lying on them for months – the testers of the great beds were an example; it took three or even four of these heavy sheets to cover them. But it had to be done because of all the dust that went swirling when the cleaners got busy with brooms and cobweb brushes.

While he was still houseman, Chris had been given the job of finding a solution to this problem of the dust sheets. What we needed was individual covers for each piece of furniture. But who was going to undertake such an enormous task? It was far too costly to be allocated to any commercial firm. Though the needleworkers among our guides might have managed some of the smaller covers, larger items seemed an intractable problem. We had to find someone who would tackle the whole job.

Chris had earlier made the acquaintance of a team of ladies

who belonged to the Norwich branch of the National Association of Decorative and Fine Arts Societies (NADFAS). Their organizer rashly remarked to Chris that she would love the chance to get her teeth into something of real use to the National Trust. Hadn't he anything he needed doing?

'Well,' said he. 'Now that you mention it . . .'

He didn't really expect that Geraldine and her team would want to take on such a vast and unglamorous chore, but to his gratitude and delight the NADFAS ladies eagerly offered their services. They undertook to make a whole set of case covers, for individual chairs, tables, long-case clocks, bureaux and bronzes, beds and chandeliers.

About three-quarters of a mile of material was patiently cut out by two volunteers under the guidance of a Trust conservator, and then each cover was tailor-made. The job was time-consuming, complicated by the addition of coloured bias binding in all the french seams, a different colour for each room. In my earlier book I briefly mentioned that the work was under way. What none of us foresaw was that it would take five years to complete this enormous task. I often wondered if the NADFAS volunteers, especially Audrey who co-ordinated the work, together with Sue, Lotte and Kirsten, ever regretted saying yes to the proposition.

During the early months of each year, the ladies came in once a week, bringing their own sewing machines, and settled in the Morning Room, a lively group of most welcome helpers. One of them worked throughout on a hand-powered Singer machine which might itself have qualified for a place among our antiques, being ninety years old. For the rest of the year, they met about once a month in one of their homes, though as one remarked, 'In my house I don't have much room to spread out with things like *this*!' and out from her bag billowed marquee-sized acres of fine cotton lawn – a cover for a four-poster bed.

In the course of this immense sewing-bee, which Chris described as one of the biggest voluntary efforts he had ever come across, one or two mistakes were inevitable, such as the moment when they came to fit a finished cover over a marble table, only to find that the statues on top of the table had been glued down, for security. They solved the problem with swift practicality – they cut two holes in the cover. During winter cleaning the statues are covered with acid-free tissue.

The NADFAS ladies always wanted to know what was happening with us, how my books were doing, and what our sons were up to. There was special hilarity one day when we told them of Kevin's impending wedding and they insisted I go and put on my outfit and model it for them; later they wanted to see the photos. They were good friends and we missed them when the work was finally finished. Thanks to their gift to Felbrigg – the generous donation of their time and skill – every piece of furniture now has its own special cover; even the chandeliers can be wrapped in vast protective bags. And the colour code is invaluable: pink for the Drawing Room, royal blue for the Cabinet, yellow for the Rose and the Yellow Bedrooms . . .

That was not quite the end of the story. Later, Chris and I were invited to be special guests at a NADFAS meeting at the Assembly Rooms in Norwich, where Chris, to his embarrassment, was publicly thanked for allowing the sewing team the privilege of undertaking this massive project! Considering we were the ones heavily in *their* debt, it was a touching gesture.

Some problems with fabric are ongoing. For instance, some of the curtains are very fragile, through the ravages of time and sunlight. A cotton pair in the Rose Bedroom is stiff, thin as paper in places, with bits liable to crack and fall off despite the careful netting which the fabric conservators have stitched to the material to hold it together. One day I went into this room to speak to a workman who was up on a ladder fixing the window. Before I could stop him, he took hold of the nearest curtain in both hands and shook it vigorously, laughing, 'Listen how it crackles! It's like plastic!'

I'm not sure whether it was the look on my face or my shriek of horror that made him turn pale and drop the curtain as if it had turned into a snake.

So the weeks passed, Easter approached, the daffodils danced on the pasture. And all the time, up in the Chinese Bedroom, in a space amid lath and plaster behind the ancient Chinese wallpaper, the dry rot mycelia were spreading ever further, silently, secretly, and still undetected . . .

Fun with film crews

In spring, the media look around for attractions to fill their 'What's On' and 'Where to Go' spots and, naturally, Trust properties are a favourite subject; they provide lovely pictures for the television audience and suggest a fine day out for the family. Chris never turned down an opportunity to get Felbrigg's name mentioned in the local press; it was all part of his plan to publicize the property and attract more people. We now have a scrap book bulging with newspaper cuttings, and our own video collection of pieces featuring Felbrigg. Which is useful: when we have visitors who look as if they might stay too late, we don't threaten them with holiday snaps, we offer to get out our Felbrigg videos!

National Trust properties are popular, too, as backgrounds for dramas, documentaries, or even advertisements. Before our time, Felbrigg was even used in a *Monty Python* sketch. Sometimes when a media company's advance party comes to view the property, of course, the place may prove not quite right for their purposes; but, if it suits them, they agree terms and sign contracts and arrange a date with the administrator for filming – another excitement to be fitted into the crowded schedule.

In the months when I was acting houseman we were expecting a film crew from the BBC's Pebble Mill studios, who were coming to film sequences for a prestigious television production of D. H. Lawrence's *The Rainbow*. Scenes were to be filmed in several locations of Norfolk, plus other places in Yorkshire and Lawrence's native Nottinghamshire. The BBC had arranged to do half a day's filming in the Hall in early March, plus a couple of days in the gardens. More outdoor scenes were to be shot in June, when summer growth would be evident. The crew would be working at Felbrigg during the day and staying in a local hotel at night. We looked forward to their company. Such extracurricular activities can be great fun, a change from everyday routine, and it is fascinating to watch experts at work.

Filming in National Trust properties is a source of valuable extra revenue, an extension of good public relations and, always, excellent publicity. It also calls for extra vigilance from house staff, whose main task is to ensure the security of the house and its contents against loss and/or damage. Some less experienced film crew personnel may not be aware of the frailty of their 'set'; they have to be reminded that our precious furniture, books and knick-knacks are not ordinary props.

In early March, a PR girl from the BBC called to say that they were sorry to cause us problems but they were behind in their schedule and would now need to fit in their Felbrigg filming in the week immediately before Easter. Oh, help! During that last week before opening to the public we hope to be getting everything straight, the rooms set out down to the smallest item, all spick and span after the long months of upheaval during the winter. Each day is fully booked, with little time for unexpected extra activities. However, realizing that the BBC would not have made the request had it not been vital, Chris agreed that the filming in the Library could take place on the Wednesday. He calculated that this would give us a day to clear up in the house and get the place back to normal before the cleaners and ourselves had a day's break on Good Friday. Outdoor filming was scheduled for Thursday and Friday, all to be completed by the time we opened on Saturday. At least, that was the plan.

The busy week began with the pre-season meeting, when all staff and volunteers gather for final messages and instructions before we open. This year, being Chris's first at the helm, was especially important for him. He wanted to emphasize his vision of everyone playing an equally important part in Felbrigg's team, be they volunteers, department managers, cleaners, shop assistants, waitresses, or full-time staff, indoors or out.

In the event, it was that same evening when the first advance vehicle from the BBC arrived – the caterer's van. 'Oh, didn't anyone explain that we'd need a day or so to set up prior to filming?' the caterer asked cheerily.

By mid-morning on Tuesday the front courtyard and the grass

area around it were crammed with huge vehicles laden with equipment, with people spilling everywhere going about their mysterious tasks. One pantechnicon had to be moved when it parked right over the ancient cellar, whose curved ceiling is only about two feet below the pea shingle. After recent alarums in Norwich, when a double-decker bus slid nose-down into a sudden hole in the road, when old mine workings decided they couldn't take the strain any more, we didn't want similar scenes at Felbrigg – some kinds of publicity we can do without.

Anyone who has ever sat through the credits of a movie or television production will have some idea of the number of people involved, a small army who all have to be fed and watered. Along with the huge lorries and vans containing technical equipment – the hardware that goes with modern lighting and sound, the cables for power, the cameras, the tracks, the props gear and the costumes – there was a mobile lavatory which parked just beneath our living room window, a large coach which doubled as a diner and meeting room, and, most important of all, the catering caravan, run by a lovely chap named Peter. We got to know him quite well as he needed constant water laid on; technicians fixed up a large-bore hose which ran all the way through our flat and out through our kitchen window – that happened to be the most convenient way of doing it. The flow was turned off last thing at night, in case of leaks, and put on again in the morning. We just had to remember to leap over the hose as we were dashing about our various duties.

Besides his mobile kitchen/servery, which was a miracle of packing with everything neatly in place and not an inch unused, Peter had a tent where he laid out all his salads and cold collations, while hot food was served from the van. His menu would have put many a café to shame, an amazing choice, which he and his assistant somehow produced daily, everything from cooked breakfasts, through smoked salmon and prawn salad to hot pies and curries, with tea and coffee available all the time. All of it looked and smelt wonderful.

While the film crew were with us, the main door of the Hall had to be kept open, which was a concern because of the visitors wandering around, walking in the park and woods; the sight of all those vehicles cluttering up the frontage brought many curious enquiries as to what was going on from spectators who waited around hoping to see something of interest. Given half a chance, some of them would have been inside the Hall.

Because Chris and I were coping alone with the house and all its varied goings-on, we had asked for extra volunteers from among our Felbrigg friends to help out with security. They, and we, were invited to have our meals from the catering wagon whenever we wished – breakfast, lunch and tea. One of our young helpers, home from college, confessed that one morning he had consumed *three* plateful of eggs, bacon and sausage from Peter's van. The rest of us were more circumspect, I think, but I confess it was luxury, in the middle of a busy day, to be supplied with a meal one didn't have to prepare oneself.

The weather was filthy during those few days, but somehow in between downpours they managed to do their outdoor filming. Indoor filming was, fortunately, confined to the Library, with its magnificent oak bookpresses and rows of leather-bound volumes: it was to play the part of the library at Nottingham University in Victorian times. But, of course, the Library is on the first floor and access to it is through the lobby, the Great Hall, the main staircase hall . . .

The weather made everything more difficult. The crew laid down plastic so that they wouldn't tramp too much wet and mud into the Hall, but with all the comings and goings some mess was inevitable. Then the setting-up took much longer than anyone had anticipated. By the Wednesday evening they hadn't shot any scenes at all. They had spent the time discussing angles, and sorting out technical problems: they wanted sunlight, but the sun stubbornly stayed in its clouded bed and, as the forecast promised only more gloom, lights had to be fixed outside the Library windows to look like sunlight.

For most of the day I was busy elsewhere in the house, but when the crew had gone, damp and frustrated, it was my job to close down behind them. They had left some electric cables trailing through the window in the Library; these had to be disconnected and coiled up out of the way before I could close the shutters. The room was full of exotic equipment – lights, cameras and trolleys – and the furniture had been rearranged into unfamiliar patterns.

Going into the Great Hall below, I discovered a chandelier on the floor – no, not one of ours, though for just a moment I feared . . . ! At second glance I saw it was a prop. The crew evidently intended to do something with it the next day. Since their ways were a mystery to me, I left it where it was, secured the house, and went up to make supper.

Later, joining Chris in the office where he was catching up with paperwork, I happened to ask him if he knew what plans the film crew had for the chandelier.

'What chandelier?' said Chris.

'The one they've left sitting on the floor in the Great Hall,' said I.

He frowned. 'I don't remember them mentioning anything about a chandelier. I'd better check.' But first, just to make sure I hadn't been dreaming, he had to unset the alarms and go down to examine the object. It proved to be extremely heavy. Where did they intend to hang it?

Back in the office, he phoned the hotel and eventually got hold of the chap he wanted. 'About this chandelier . . .'

'Yes, that's right. We're going to hang it in the Library tomorrow, for a more authentic touch. They used to have chandeliers in Nottingham University library, you know.'

'How are you intending to hang it?' Chris asked. 'There's no fitting in the ceiling.'

'No, that's all right, we're going to suspend it from a pole spanning the room, with both ends resting on the tops of the bookcases.'

Now, Felbrigg Library's bookpresses are topped by handsome oak pediments, which have been there for many years and which could easily be damaged by something heavy resting on them. 'I can't let you do that,' said Chris. 'I've just tried to lift that chandelier and it's no lightweight.'

'It won't hurt,' said the man. 'I know the chandelier's heavy, but we're going to hang it from an aluminium pole.'

'So?'

'Well, aluminium's very light – it's only the pole that will be touching your book-cases, after all.'

Whether he was really so naïve as to be unaware that a heavy object suspended from a pole puts all its weight on that pole, or whether he hoped Chris was unversed in the laws of physics, I do not know, but I was there when this conversation took place so I can vouch for Chris's end of it, at least.

'You've got to be joking,' he said. 'I can't let you put that sort of weight on those pediments. I'm sorry, but it's my job to protect the place.'

When the technician realized that his arguments about the lightness of the pole weren't having any effect, he had another idea: 'How about if we bring an extending pole, brace it between the walls and hang the chandelier from that?'

'That'll need so much force you'll probably knock the walls out!' said Chris. 'No, I'm sorry. If you're going to hang the chandelier you'll have to find some way of doing it without risking the fabric of the place.'

The man argued, but Chris remained adamant. He had to: Felbrigg was his first concern, its safety not to be risked for a fleeting moment on film, however artistically relevant.

In the end, they dispensed with the chandelier altogether and hired some lovely old oil lamps from a lamp shop in the village of Stiffkey a few miles along the coast. They added a wonderful warm ambience to the scene and I don't think the chandelier was missed.

Another idea was to give the Library a misty look, such as you often see when cloisters are filmed, with sunlight slanting through soft drifting mist. This effect does give a pleasant texture to the picture, in appropriate places. But before they did the filming Chris wanted to know how they would create the effect.

'We've got a smoke machine,' he was told.

'And how does it work?'

'It puffs out a light smoke. Nothing to worry about. It disperses completely in a few minutes. We use it all the time. We've used it in hundreds of different locations. Perfectly harmless.'

'Can you give me a demonstration?' said Chris. 'Somewhere well out of harm's way – just in case.'

So off they trooped, in the uncertain light of another mournful, dank day, down to the far end of the Red Corridor, past the shop and into the disused 'lock-up' area. There, they showed Chris how the machine worked. Smoke began to issue forth . . .

Bare seconds later, every fire alarm in the house was screaming. Chris and his companions guessed what was causing the noise, but I and the other helpers knew only that the alarm had sounded and we must go into our precautionary routine. Which meant clearing the house.

Neither the technicians nor the actors waiting in full costume were terribly pleased to be ushered out into miserable drizzle and made to wait until I could ensure that there was no fire, and who could blame them? But, after the example of Hampton Court, where only a couple of years before fatalities had occurred when fire broke out, we could not afford to take chances. When we explained how important it was, our new friends understood and took it in good part, but it was yet another disruption for them. And, of course, Chris was obliged to forbid the use of the smoke machine.

Going along the Red Corridor later, I found it full of a beautiful veiling mist, which hung there for hours. When it eventually dispersed it left everything coated in a thin film of oily stuff. I know, because I spent most of Good Friday washing that film off the many panes of glass in the tall windows all down that long corridor.

Despite these odd hiccups, we had a happy few days playing host to the BBC crew. They were a friendly crowd. It was interesting to see them at work and admire the pains they took over every detail, sometimes working for hours to set up a shot that lasted only seconds on the screen.

The same crew returned for a few days in June, when they shot several scenes in the walled garden and its greenhouses. Some plants were specially bought in for the filming; a rose bush was moved because in one shot there was too much greenhouse and not enough foliage; and the props team built a lot of staging which they left for our gardeners to use. Our head gardener, Ted Bullock, was pleased about that.

Less pleased was the director, when a passer-by driving

through the park stopped right in shot and refused to budge despite shouts and wavings. He didn't stir until someone went over to talk to him. Wonderful what some folk will do for a crinkly tenner.

Naturally we told everyone to be sure to watch *The Rainbow* when it was televised that December over three Sunday evenings. We watched it avidly ourselves, delighted with the glimpses of the Library, the greenhouse scenes, and one lovely shot of Ursula, played by Imogen Stubbs, seated in a gnarled old apple tree by our garden gate. What we hadn't anticipated – rather stupidly, considering that D. H. Lawrence also wrote *Lady Chatterley's Lover* – was that the story would include several explicit sexual episodes, including some lesbian interludes and one nude love scene when the pair were standing in a lake.

'Was that the Felbrigg lake?' people asked later.

'Yes, it was. I did a lot of underwater work in that scene!' Chris joked.

Some of our guides didn't have much to say about it. I don't think they were amused at our recommending it as suitable viewing!

However, I'm sure that some of the earlier inhabitants of Felbrigg would have been diverted by it all. Staunch Protestants they may have been, most of them, but they had their share of red-blooded *roués*.

Felbrigg folk

The story of Felbrigg goes back to Norman times and the powerful Bigod family, the first Earls of Norfolk under William the Conqueror. A minor member of this dynasty settled in north Norfolk and took the name de Felbrigg from the place where he built his manor house. Nothing now remains, or is known, of this early building, except that one of the cellars – the one over which the BBC pantechnicon had parked – may have been an undercroft to it. More of that later when we visit the cellars in detail.

The first famous member of the de Felbrigg family was Sir Simon, who was standard bearer to Richard II; his wife, Lady

What we hadn't anticipated was that the story included
several explicit sexual episodes . . .

Margaret, was cousin and lady-in-waiting to Richard's queen, Anne of Bohemia. So the de Felbriggs were important members of the court. Lady Margaret died in 1416 and her grieving husband ordered the making of the commemorative brass which may still be seen in the church. Considered to be one of the finest brasses in England, it shows both Lady Margaret and Sir Simon, almost life-size, with a gap for the date of his death when it came. He evidently intended to be buried beside her. However, the space remains empty on the brass to this day. Like other men whose schemes are doomed to 'gang aft agley', Sir Simon married again; when he died his second wife, who came from Norwich, had him buried in the great church of the Dominican Priory in the city, and herself alongside him twenty years later.

After them, the manor of Felbrigg passed into other hands and was eventually bought by John Wyndham, in whose family it remained for many generations, though not without turmoil. The Wyndhams appear to have been a quarrelsome lot, arguing amongst themselves and with their neighbours, especially the Pastons, with litigation constantly being threatened or enacted. One claimant to the estate arrived while the squire was out, battered his way into the lady of the manor's bedroom, dragged her out by the hair and threw her from the house.

When these Norfolk Wyndhams petered out, the estate was taken over by a branch of the family from Orchard in Somerset, a scion of whom changed the Felbrigg family name to Windham, with an 'i'. He, Thomas Windham, was responsible for beginning the building of the house as we know it today, with its Great Hall and its stately Jacobean front, work which started around 1620. Only half a century later, William Windham I ordered the building of the west wing, which by contrast looks almost Georgian in character. If you were shown photographs of Felbrigg from the south, and then from the west, you could be forgiven for thinking it was two different houses. But somehow the styles blend into a pleasing whole.

Over the years the house was altered inside as fashions changed and new ideas of comfort and convenience came in, while outside new wings and outhouses arose, the last being the stable block. Then in the 1860s came the nadir of its fortunes when the young squire, William Frederick 'Mad' Windham, squandered his inheritance with the aid of a lady of the *demi-monde*, whom he had the bad judgement to marry. The estate was forfeit and had to be sold.

By great good fortune, it was bought just as it stood by a merchant from Norwich, one John Kitton, who changed his name to Ketton. He must have been a sensitive man for he left the house and its contents just as they had developed over the years. He didn't start redecorating, or ordering gaudy new furniture, or swapping the pictures around: he left Felbrigg with its character intact. His own portrait is tucked modestly away in a corner of the Morning Room.

John Ketton's son, Robert (1854–1935), lived into old age unmarried, with the estate gradually going to ruin around him. Interested only in the woods and the shooting, he lived in a couple of rooms of the house, with a cook and butler to look after him, and the rest of the Hall was left to moulder. His oldest sister, Rachel Anna, had married Thomas Wyndham-Cremer, a direct descendant of Sir John Wyndham of Orchard, and when Robert Ketton died the estate came to Rachel Anna's grandson, thus bringing the story full circle, back into the Wyndham family. Under the terms of John Ketton's will, the new owner changed his name to Ketton-Cremer.

For details of this and all other tales of Felbrigg's inhabitants, I recommend *Felbrigg, the story of a house*, which was written by the last squire, the historian Robert Wyndham Ketton-Cremer. He spent the last few years of his life preparing the house for its eventual gift to the nation, on his death in 1969. He had a vision of how he wanted the house presented – as a home – and that is how we tried to keep it, more or less as he left it, as if the squire had simply stepped out for a while. His magazines and books still lie on the tables; his writing things are on his desk; the books he loved remain.

I believe it's that special 'homely' quality that makes people come back time and time again to Felbrigg. Those who love it do so with a proprietorial passion. It has a unique charm that ought to be preserved if it's not to become just another clone of a country house. The National Trust has a difficult path to walk between providing all the mod cons that today's visitor demands and destroying the uniqueness of its properties. The choices are not easy.

The south front gets a facelift

One of these hard decisions had to be made when it came to restoring the south front of the house. This, the original Jacobean part of Felbrigg, was built with three stately bays lifting right up through two tall storeys to the parapets where, on a kind of long balcony outside the attics, one can stand and watch the world from enormous height. Viewed from the front of the house, the left-hand bay contains, on the ground floor, some of the windows which light the Great Hall, while the windows above look out from the Library. The central bay holds the entrance porch of the main house and, above it, on a mezzanine level, a tiny room in the administrator's flat (the room I used as a study). Above that again lies the 'solar', another small room-with-a-view which leads off the present Book Room. The right-hand bay has the Morning Room windows at the lowest level, and above them lies the grandest room in the administrator's flat, which we used as an occasional sitting room.

This oldest part of the house contained the original great hall, a screens passage, and a buttery, possibly with a solar above. In an age of communal living, when family, retainers and servants all ate and slept together, the solar provided some privacy for the ladies. There were also cellars beneath, used as kitchens and for storage.

The early Jacobean manor was built of red brick, but as tastes changed with the years it was variously colour-washed in brilliant white lime, or red ochre, or mustard yellow – difficult to visualize when we are used to its faded render-and-redbrick façade, weathered but somehow dignified in its decaying magnificence.

As a final conceit by a Windham squire who desired his house to appear to be made of stone instead of brick, the façade was rendered with stucco – sometimes called Roman cement – and scored in squares. This pretension was, perhaps, a pity, for the stucco had to be applied so thinly in places that for years now it has been flaking and cracking, bits falling off. Some people find the effect charming; others say it looks tatty. Still others argue that the stucco should be stripped completely, or replaced.

Our regional historic building representative, land agent, and building managers met together with the architect to discuss the problem. In their turn they were advised by one of the many committees which exist inside the Trust. In the event, no one could decide exactly what to do for the long-term best. Which period of Felbrigg's long history were they hoping to re-create with this facelift? The red brick era (but the brick is soft and weathering badly where it is already exposed)? The white, red or yellow wash periods? Or should they completely re-cover it in bright new stucco – at the risk of making the house resemble an old lady in too much make-up? In the end, they decided simply to stabilize the front as it was, so that it shouldn't deteriorate further. It was a compromise but, many of us thought, a sensible decision. If they had done anything else, they would have been bound to upset *someone*.

Up on the roof

The work of stabilization brought more teams of workmen to Felbrigg, first a pair of scaffolders who, with much clattering and banging, began to erect scaffold poles and 'deals' (planks) around the front of the house. This being an obvious temptation to burglars, more trusty men came and fixed warning lamps and klaxons designed to activate whenever anyone (or anything) came too close to the Hall out of hours. Fortunately they organized the beams high enough so they wouldn't be set off by every passing rabbit.

While the work was in progress, we had a team of National Trust Volunteers staying in the base camp over the stables. These stalwarts arrive now and then to help out with work around the park and woods, perhaps cleaning out part of the lake, or reinforcing pathways. Our own north Norfolk branch do a lot of useful work. Once they cleared out years of debris from the ice house and, in our time, when the local NT Volunteers' chairman, Roger, mentioned that his team would love to do some work in the house if needed, Chris had them in to sweep out the cellars. On other occasions they helped us by acting as ushers for evening events.

This time a couple of the visiting volunteers, returning late from the local pub (it's a long walk), cut close across the front of the Hall. Too close. Spotlights glared out. Sirens wailed. We leapt from our bed and went running to see two sheepish figures lit up like escapees from Colditz, waving their arms and mouthing against the clamour, 'Sorry! Sorry!'

'Well, move away!' we yelled at them, near deafened. 'Move back and it'll stop!'

They did, and it did. Phew! Blissful silence. The pair trundled off, calling again, 'Sorry!' through chokes of laughter.

The temptation to replay the joke proved too much. Over the next couple of nights, the lights and sirens started up two or three times, only to fade as we rushed to the window. Thankfully, the hilarity factor soon wore thin.

Going up to the roof on a summer's evening became one of our small pleasures, a perk we especially savoured after a long hot day. The stairs in our new flat led right up to the attics at the front of the house, where you can climb on to the parapet through a small dormer window – if you're limber enough. Once or twice we took a salad supper up there, with a bottle of wine, and stood viewing the world feeling like lords of all we surveyed, watching the cars drive slowly by as people enjoyed the sight of the house, or families came walking, playing ball, or couples walked their dogs. And slowly the sun sank, a glory of gold and flame over the woods, leaving the evening star brightening in a pale sky.

The roof was always a place of escape, an oasis of quiet whatever the time of day or night. Often Chris would go up there last thing before retiring. Sometimes the stars were out, brilliant with no town lights to fade them, the constellations standing out clear. Sometimes the moon was full, lighting the park, and a mist might be creeping under the trees, the cows like black statues standing up to their knees in it, as if wading in a silver river. You might hear an owl call, and see it swoop on graceful wings, a pale ghost in the night, or hear a fox bark, or watch the bats come silently flitting . . . By night the roof is a place of mystery, where you can spy on creatures of the dark.

By day, the roof has other attractions. Sun-worshippers could lie up there and soak up the heat – if they had the time. But even given only a few minutes you can recharge your spiritual batteries up there, far above the everyday hustle.

Chris was taking the air and briefly enjoying the peace of the parapets one bright morning when two ladies appeared below him, sauntering slowly up to the front courtyard gate, which bears the notice declaring that the house is closed. Neither of them had noticed Chris, but their voices floated clearly up to him.

'I told you they were closed today,' one of them said.

Her companion sighed. 'Oh dear. Are you sure? Won't they be open later?'

From his perch above, Chris said loudly, 'I'm afraid we're always closed on Tuesdays.'

The ladies jumped. One of them glanced behind her, the other one stared up, not at the house but straight into the blue sky, saying, 'Who was that?' as if she believed the Almighty himself had proclaimed.

'I'm afraid we're closed today,' Chris said again, causing more consternation. It was some while before they got the direction of his voice and at last spied him standing there thirty feet or so above them, which afforded them some amusement – and not a little relief.

So temptingly peaceful is the roof, especially on a hot, busy day, that Chris occasionally went out during his regular after-noon rounds when the Hall was open to visitors. One Sunday nearly proved his undoing.

At that height it was more windy than he had anticipated and as he climbed out of the little window it slammed shut behind him. The latch, which sticks a bit, dropped into place, locking him out. He could have waited to be found, I suppose, but it might have been hours before we thought to look for him there

– a tempting thought for him, probably. Or he might have called down to a visitor, to ask him to alert the ticket seller to fetch someone to the rescue. However, as luck would have it, there were no visitors nearby at that moment.

But there *was* the scaffolding. It offered a secure platform, its top stage not far below the parapet, with ladders leading down to the stages below. He could be down to the ground in minutes without troubling anyone.

So over he climbed, walked along to the nearest ladder, and went down to the next level. Only then, as he looked further down, did he realize that, alas, the lowest ladders had been removed. Since the workmen were not on duty on a Sunday they had naturally left their scaffolding secure against assault from casual climbers. (For some reason, they hadn't anticipated that the administrator might need an escape route from his own roof!)

Fortunately, as Chris could now see, the next stage down was level with the Library windows, which were open to the breeze, and there was a final ladder by which he could reach them. His appearance outside the window caused quite a stir among the visitors in the Library, though the room warden, Harry, laughed uproariously as he helped Chris inside.

Afterwards, Harry derived a lot of comic mileage telling how the administrator had evolved a cunning new way of making sure his staff behaved themselves: he didn't lurk behind doorways, he spied on them from outside the windows – even on the first floor.

In sickness . . .

Just after the Hall opened that year, while I was houseman, Chris fell sick with what the doctor said was a virus; the patient should stay in bed for a fortnight. Easy to say, but how could he, when there were only the two of us on full-time duty and I certainly wasn't competent to run the house single-handed?

Chris coped by staying in bed during the morning, with the phone beside him, groggily taking messages while I managed the jobs around the house. In season, fortunately, everything has a routine and everyone is in the swing of it; hiccups and unexpected problems don't seem so bad when there are other staff around to help, and we were fortunate in having a good back-up team. In the afternoon, Chris forced himself to get dressed and came down to greet the room wardens and see the open session underway, then he went up to the office and did the necessary paperwork while I stayed round the house to deal with whatever occurred. There is always something – a driver parking in the wrong place must be asked to move; someone may want information beyond a room warden's scope; the shop can run out of change, or receive a complaint; a restaurant customer may need placating. A hundred different problems crop up. Occasionally it was something I couldn't deal with myself, so as usual the final resort was to Chris, however ill he was feeling. And at the end of the day he had the cash to reconcile and return sheets to fill out – he was the only one capable of doing that efficiently. I might have tried it, but only with tuition, and Chris didn't have the energy to teach me.

In a way, however, that fraught period proved personally satisfying for me. It certainly boosted my confidence when I found myself obliged to attend, and able to cope with, site meetings concerning the building of a new restaurant in the stable block. I also once found myself loudly berating a pair of recalcitrant scaffolders. (What, mild-mannered me? I could hardly believe it myself!)

On another occasion, the architect and buildings team approached a site meeting with some caution because they feared they had upset one of the contractors, a man reputed to have a terrible temper. Oh dear, here he came . . . Who was going to speak to him first? 'I'll do it,' said I, and went off to meet the man with smiles, cheerful greetings, and sincere apologies about the misunderstanding that had occurred. We were all so sorry he had been upset. He gave me a sidelong look, then relaxed and sighed – couldn't withstand my female wiles, poor chap. I do not apologize for using what little I had of middle-aged charm to defuse what might have been an awkward situation. It's called diplomacy, is it not?

Unhappily for Chris, his illness continued for six weeks, not two as the doctor had predicted. 'These undefined viruses aren't predictable,' we were told. Nor do they respond to medication. Chris developed a horrible hacking cough which lingered for months and still recurs whenever his strength is low. In fact, three years later an X-ray revealed a shadow on his lung and after a week or two of sheer terror (for me, anyway) we were told that it was an old scar – he had had TB not long ago, hadn't he been aware of it? We can only assume that this was the 'virus' that made him so ill for those long weeks.

One morning when the alarm clock roused me out of deep sleep, I went downstairs in a daze to turn off the security system before letting the cleaners in. I was so exhausted that I got the routine wrong and set off the alarms. They screamed their warnings at my aching head, and the great siren on the roof went off like wartime, alerting half the county before I could fumble for the right switch and turn the noise off. Blessed relief. Wonderful, echoing silence.

A short while later I answered the door to two stern-looking policeman who were not at all pleased at being called out on a false alarm because of some stupid female. 'Don't let it happen again!' they warned. 'If you cry wolf too often, we might not come when you need us. Next time, call and let us know it's a mistake.'

'Sorry, officer. I was half asleep.' I felt like a naughty little girl.

Mark, the assistant gardener, happened to be outside the door as the policemen departed. He gave me an understanding grin. 'They didn't arrest you, then?'

One evening soon after this, when Chris had crawled into bed after finishing the cash, the alarms went off again. Having checked which area was affected, I cautiously went to see what was happening and, finding no signs of intruders, returned to the flat to reassure Chris and to phone the police to tell them not to turn out. Occasional faults did happen. Usually the alarms would reset without too many problems. This time, they wouldn't.

Since the property must not be left unprotected for longer than necessary, I called the alarm company and was told that their duty engineer was miles away in the south of the county. He would probably be with us around ten, or soon after. While waiting, thoroughly on edge by this time and needing a breath of air, I went out for a run in the damp night – having locked the Hall securely behind me. At last I saw lights coming down the driveway. Yes, it was the engineer. Hooray.

I led him through the pitch-dark Hall by torchlight – Felbrigg had no electricity until the 1950s and then, to avoid damaging the ornate ceilings, power was brought to sockets low down in skirting or floorboards; the state rooms are lit only by standard lamps, which, of course, are unplugged every evening, for safety's sake. If, therefore, you want to go through the rooms at night, either you rummage around trying to plug in lamps as you go, or you simply use a torch. The torch is less hassle, but beyond its meagre light great shadows fill the empty spaces around the walls and under the high ceilings; furniture squats in darkness, sending more shadows looming and hunching; a mirror reflects a ghostly movement – your own, you hope.

That evening, I led the engineer through the darkling rooms and finally showed him where the fault was. As I turned away to plug in a lamp so that he could see what he was doing, this tall, muscular, healthy young man said in a voice hushed with horror, 'Good Lord! How on earth do you stand it? I wouldn't live here for a thousand pounds a week!'

Funny, I'd never thought of it like that. It was Felbrigg. It was my home. And, much as I'd have liked to see one of the ghosts that some claim abide there, I never saw or felt a thing. Perhaps I'm just not sensitive to such vibes.

Man on the scaffolding

The scaffolding remained in place for most of that season, blighting the face of Felbrigg but providing a necessary perch, not only for the men who were stabilizing the façade: others were renovating the leaded windows; some had jobs to do on the roof; and yet others had been repairing and repainting the stone sundial which lives on the south front. The scaffolding was also the scene of a nasty accident when one young man, working

'. . . I wouldn't live here for a thousand pounds a week!'

alone against all the rules, fell twenty feet on to the shingle. The morning ticket seller, dispensing garden tickets, heard him fall and summoned us to help. Happily, the young man recovered, though it was a long, painful time for him.

It was well into autumn before the scaffolding could be taken down. By that time, our new houseman Eddie had joined us, but the day the scaffolders came to remove their planks and poles was a Tuesday – his day off – so once again Chris and I were alone, with only the cleaners in the house.

After the scaffolders' lorry edged into the front courtyard, a little clattering and banging ensued, then . . . silence. A short time later they were at the back door, saying that they couldn't go any further until the security lights and sirens were removed, and that wasn't their job because the security fixings belonged to the electrical sub-contractors, whose prerogative it was to dismantle them.

Chris phoned the firm, but all of their men were out on other jobs and no one could be found to do this small chore. So Chris decided he would have to do it himself. He was anxious to have the scaffolding taken away, and for the Hall to look its usual elegant self again. Meanwhile, the two scaffolders had retired to the cab of their lorry for mugs of tea and cigarettes, apparently prepared to sit there all day.

Chris's earlier adventure on the scaffolding had worried me when I'd heard about it. This time I knew what he was intending, and I also knew there was frost on the scaffolding, so the planks and poles were slippery. Two men had put those lights and cables up, so dismantling them single-handed was not going to be easy. What was worse, the lower ladders were not in place, so Chris decided to climb out through a window. I went with him and watched, fuming at his stubbornness.

'Well, I can't let them sit out there all day waiting,' was his reply. 'Besides, I want to be rid of this ugly scaffolding. It's been up all season.'

I have seldom been so angry, or felt so impotent, or so afraid, even while I admired his determination to get the job done. I went racing down the stairs and out into the damp courtyard, where the scaffolders were enjoying their break.

'Are you just going to sit there and let him do it on his own?' I yelled at them. 'Can't you even lend him a hand? I know it's not strictly your job, but it's not his, either, and—'

To give the men their due, I don't think they had realized what Chris was up to. Alerted by my wifely concern, they leapt out of their lorry and at once put up the ladders and went to help him, much to my relief.

3

Close encounters of the gatepost kind

Local rubbish was collected by a private company whose vehicle one day had a slight coming-together with a brick gatepost at Sexton's Lodge, the back entrance to Felbrigg Hall, where the driveway runs into the narrow lane of Lion's Mouth. Alerted to the problem, Chris called in the trusty men from Bullens, the local building firm, who do a great deal of work for the Trust. They took off the dislodged capping stone and the few rows of loosened bricks and piled them neatly on the ground until their schedule allowed them to come and repair it, which wouldn't be for a week or three since their work diary was full, they informed us. The gatepost looked unsightly, but that couldn't be helped.

Not long afterwards, in the middle of a blazing hot afternoon when the Hall was swarming with visitors, we had word that one of the lorries coming to Home Farm had half demolished one of the gateposts at the *main* entrance. Chris left me in charge while he went to investigate and found the top of the gatepost leaning at a precarious angle, held up only by the fact that the gate attached to it, which had been wide open, was now at an angle, its corner digging deep into the ground as it supported the weight of the tall, brick-built gatepost. It threatened to topple at any minute; Chris daren't risk having it fall on any of our visitors. Our new woodsman, Gary, came along and stopped the traffic coming through by directing cars round to the back entrance at Lion's Mouth, a detour of at least two miles.

Luckily the gardeners, Ted and Mark, had also heard of the problem and they, too, turned up at the gate to help – in times of trouble, everyone at Felbrigg pitched in. Chris came back to the Hall to tell us what was happening and enlisted the aid of one of the room wardens, a sturdy lady named Betty, who went with him back to the main gate to direct traffic.

The hold-up on the road outside brought the police to investigate. They lent some of their fluorescent jackets, one of which Betty wore to give her extra authority as she spoke to drivers and told them how to get round to the Lion's Mouth.

A couple of coaches, sent off round the lanes, came back half an hour later saying they couldn't find the lane, so Ted and Mark started to board any coaches that came, to ride 'shotgun' with them and guide them to the rear gate, while Chris, Betty and the police manned the main gate.

Once again Bullens' men came, this time in a hurry, to perform the difficult task of dismantling the teetering brickwork without damaging it or the wrought-iron gate.

Betty said later that she had had a marvellous time. Best day she'd spent in an age!

What our visitors thought, having to 'follow-my-leader' by the tortuous route to Sexton's Lodge, only to see that the *back* gatepost was in pieces, too, I do not know. Wasn't it Oscar Wilde who commented that, 'To lose one . . . may be regarded as misfortune; to lose both looks like carelessness'? He was talking about parents, but the same applies. And, considering the superstition that misfortunes come in threes, we were concerned for the third entry gate. Tucked away in the back of beyond, it leads only to a farm track. The last we heard, those gates remained intact.

Wedding bells at Felbrigg

Chris's hopes of expanding possibilities at Felbrigg were shared by Joan, who was equally keen to try new ideas. The spring of 1989 saw the beginning of work on a new restaurant which would greatly expand our facilities and give Joan the chance to cater for extra functions. But, months before the new Park Restaurant opened, Chris and Joan presided over another 'first' for Felbrigg – the wedding of a local girl.

The young couple wanted to be married in Felbrigg's picturesque church, have photographs taken with the Hall as a background, reception drinks in the Morning Room and the wedding breakfast in the Old Kitchen. Planning had been going on for months, both Joan and Chris meeting with the bride and her parents several times. The only thing we couldn't guarantee was the weather.

However, when the day arrived (a Friday in May, when the Hall was closed to the public) it proved warm and sunny.

It being officially our day off, I stayed in the flat trying not to display my curiosity, though I couldn't resist peeping through various windows to see what was going on. After all, this was the first wedding we had hosted and if it went well it could lead to other bookings. I heard the church bell ringing and saw the cars making through the park towards the church half a mile from the house.

Eventually, the service over, a horse and carriage, smartly accoutred with ribbons flying, came clopping up the drive and into the front courtyard – a real replay of history. How many other brides had arrived in like style over the centuries? I watched unashamedly from the bay window in our huge sitting room, enjoying the spectacle.

As ever, photographs were taken by the dozen: the happy couple with the pony and trap, in it and climbing out of it, standing by it . . . outside the main door . . . with parents, without parents, bridesmaids, page boy . . . It was a beautiful day with just enough breeze to set the women clutching at their hats and skirts and they all seemed to be enjoying the ambience of the old house.

Chris was waiting to welcome the wedding party and to equip the ladies with plastic tips for their stiletto heels (which are murder to wooden floors). He found himself down on his knees, lifting the bride's hem so he could fit her shoes with protective plastic, and, happening to note that her garter had slipped down, he caught himself starting to slide it up her calf.

'Whoops, sorry!'

She laughed, and her parents, who had got to know Chris and his sense of humour, thought it a great joke. He was, after all, old enough to be the girl's father – at least! Only the groom remained unsmiling. Chris wondered afterwards if perhaps the young man had feared he might be going to demand his *droit de seigneur*!

Later I saw the party having more photographs taken in the sunlight of the Rose Garden below, against a background of the lilac and white drapery of the wisteria which hangs along the wall and looks so lovely every spring. They could not have had a more perfect setting.

The bride's father, having Italian connections, had made paper swans to sit by every place at the dining tables, each swan bearing a flurry of net containing a few sugared almonds – a charming custom which, he assured us, was common in Italy. When he sent up a spare swan for me I was touched. I still have it. (The almonds remain inside the net – I don't want to spoil it.) It's a lovely memento of a wonderful day, the first of several weddings to take place at Felbrigg while we were there.

An unexpected postscript to that story came over a year later, when Chris and I, on a day off, went to the great Worstead Festival. This event is held every year, when the whole village seems to get involved in opening gardens and farms, holding craft exhibitions and a huge show on the village field, and, of course, weaving demonstrations in the church – Worstead is the home of the original worsted cloth and weaving is still a great tradition. As we strolled round one of the barns where people were showing off their crafts, Chris recognized, sitting amid a display of photographs, the chap who had done the pictures for that first Felbrigg wedding. In fact, there in pride of place by his stall, on an easel, was a blown-up version of one of the shots of the horse and carriage, with the bride and groom posing happily, the stately frontage of the Hall behind them.

And, from an upper window, peered the pale but unmistakable face of the administrator's wife, looking down on the scene like some forlorn ghost.

'It's me!' I cried. 'Look!'

The photographer's flabber had never been so gasted. 'I hadn't noticed that before,' he said with a frown. 'Thanks for telling me. I shall have to air-brush it out.'

The wedding was not the only new event to take place under Chris's lead. On another 'closed' day we hosted a 'Volvo Day' for a local car sales firm. They set their huge banners by the courtyard gates and brought a range of shining new Volvos to stand on the shingle while invited customers took test drives and enjoyed drinks and snacks in the Morning Room. That made a change, especially when the owner of the sales firm offered each of us a drive in one of the gleaming cars. Chris went off in the largest saloon while Joan, and Eileen, her assistant, went for the sportiest model.

Another day we provided the venue for a meeting of a group of pig-breeders and their wives. 'Pig-breeders?' one of our guides exclaimed in astonishment on hearing the news. 'In our Morning Room? But what about their muddy boots? And the smell . . .'

He will be relieved to know that the pig-men came dressed in smart suits, smelling not of ordure but of expensive after-shave.

Nights at the opera

Visitors gazing at the books that line the walls of Felbrigg's Library have been known to comment that the family must have been very fond of music: 'All these books about opera.' In this context, of course, the word is Latin and means simply 'works' by the author. But not all of us are Latin scholars. I remember once being told an amusing tale by the staff of another National Trust property, where visitors kept referring to the ancient Roman underground heating system as the 'holocaust'. I couldn't understand why this was so funny − until then, I'd never come across the proper word, *hypocaust*, either. But that's by the way.

The families of Felbrigg may well have enjoyed music. There's a Bechstein grand piano in the Morning Room and presumably someone could play it − one of the five jolly Ketton girls, perhaps, with her sisters singing along, back in the 1860s. But, on the subject of opera, we were about to give the ghosts a treat . . .

Friday concerts, usually held every month during the open season, are a regular part of Felbrigg's attractions. However, during Chris's first July as administrator we played host to a new venture: three evenings of opera, held *al fresco* in the grass courtyard. These had been planned some time before, so Chris had had no part in arranging them; it was simply his task to do the final organizing and preside over the evenings.

When he examined logistics, the project seemed a trifle ambitious: in order to cover costs, we should need to sell two hundred tickets for each of the three nights. Monthly concerts easily sell out seventy seats, which is all the Morning Room can hold, but it was going to be difficult to find six hundred people, in that small area of rural Norfolk, willing to buy tickets for two short, little-known operas. The problem at Felbrigg is that half of the catchment area is sea, and not many Cromer crabs and fishes will buy tickets for classical music evenings.

The company, Claxton Opera, under their director Richard White, were to present Thomas Arne's *The Cooper* and Pergolesi's *La Serva Padrona* (The Maid as Mistress). These one-act gems of wit and musical delight were to be performed either side of an interval for drinks, the evening ending with a salad supper. Richard and the company, with their friends to help, had agreed to do most of the setting up themselves since they knew how short-handed we were. Their task involved erecting, in the grass courtyard behind the house, a semicircle of staging. Here, seating for the audience was placed, covered by a framework of scaffold poles over which tarpaulins could be draped if it rained during a performance. Scenery appeared against the wall under the courtyard clock, and a red and white striped tent, open on one side, would shelter the orchestra. In the event of a downpour, the singers would catch the worst of it: their changing room was a hundred yards away, in part of the old stables which was then the games room of the base camp (it had an old ping-pong table in it).

Since the Old Kitchen tearoom, the only catering facility we then had, couldn't have coped with the hoped-for crowds, Joan and her team prepared to serve interval drinks and post-performance suppers in a marquee close by the Hall. All this activity, and then the final rehearsals, provided a colourful outlook for the tenants and staff whose quarters lay off the grass courtyard.

On the first evening the audience was a bit thin. Some of them had dressed up for the occasion, others had come sensibly wrapped and a few brought cushions and blankets – wisely, since in fading sunset the July evening was cool. We were a little late starting, vainly hoping that some more people might turn up to buy tickets at the gate, but before long Chris was making his welcoming speech and introducing the evening.

Orchestra and singers were on form, and all was going well with *La Serva Padrona* until Chris realized that, because of the late start, the opera was going to continue just past nine o'clock, and on the hour the courtyard clock would strike.

'Quick!' he instructed. 'Stop the clock. Stop the clock!'

Easily said. Not so easily done when you have to find the right set of keys, let yourself through several locked doors, climb a rickety, twisting stairway and then try to halt a mechanism which . . .

Too late.

We loved to hear the clock mark off the Felbrigg hours, but that night it drowned part of the final aria. Bong . . . ! Bong . . . ! Nine loud, slow times. Still, it created extra amusement and as the audience applauded the valiant singers and went off for their interval drinks they were laughing and chatting animatedly.

On that dry evening the sky remained light and the weather was mild. During the interval people wandered off down the drive and across the park with their glasses of wine, admiring the view of the Hall with the moon rising above it. Some went so far that Chris had to summon them back with a handbell.

The second opera, *The Cooper*, received an equally warm response and afterwards the company enjoyed well-earned accolades over supper with the audience. For us, left to clear up afterwards, it meant another long day, but as Chris and I wearily climbed the stairs we felt it had been worth it. Another first for Felbrigg.

Next evening the concert began on time and should, we

hoped, end shortly before the clock chimed. We would have stopped it, but with its delicate old mechanism it wasn't practical, or wise, so we kept our fingers crossed.

The trouble was, chatting with the audience as they arrived, we had laughed about the previous evening's misfortune, not realizing what effect it would have. As the climax of the first opera drew near, most eyes were riveted on the clock as the big hand moved closer to the vertical. Oh, the tension! Never have singers had so rapt an audience. You could feel breath being held. Which would get there first – the final notes of the final chorus, or the inexorable clock? Tick . . . tock . . .

The singers won – just. As the orchestra played its conclusion the clock began to strike. And a hearty, hilarious cheer went up from the audience.

But it was the last night which, to us, was the best. On the last night, it rained.

We had sold more tickets for that final performance but, as the audience arrived, a mist-fine drizzle started. Umbrellas went up. Blankets were draped Indian-style over heads. We hoped, for a while, that it would pass. When it didn't, Chris decided that the tarpaulins would have to be pulled over the framework roof above the seating.

The entire audience joined in, standing up to reach above their heads, tugging and heaving at the heavy material. The Dunkirk spirit prevailed. We all felt as if we were sharing an adventure in adversity. A drop of rain can't deter Britishers, after all. If it did, we'd be in a sorry state.

Going out to make his usual welcoming peroration, Chris took with him an umbrella – one of several left behind by absent-minded visitors. This one happened to be of the folding kind. You press a button and it opens out in three stages. Click, click, click! Like a magician, or a clown. The audience responded with cheers and applause, taking it as part of the entertainment, setting the seal on a final night which, despite the continuing drizzle, developed a wonderfully warm atmosphere of mutual enjoyment. The singers got a bit wet, but they, too, were carried away by the emotion that had built up between them and their audience and, when the evening ended, everyone agreed it had been a great event. So what if it hadn't made a huge profit? Money is not the only thing to be gained, though the accountants would have us believe otherwise.

Some of the people who came to the operas had not been to visit Felbrigg before, but later they came back to see us by daylight and recall some of the incidents of those July evenings. Some of them became regulars, coming to see the Hall or attending concerts and other functions. We like to think that our own enthusiasm rubbed off in our contact with these visitors and all the others we met over the years. It was what we had hoped for, to build a steadily increasing group of people for whom Felbrigg was a house where they knew they could rely on a friendly welcome every time they came.

Biggles drops in

Another summer ... Picture a balmy Sunday evening in June, peaceful after a busy open day full of the usual small dramas. The Hall closed its doors at five thirty; the room wardens departed; the ticket seller, recruiters, shop manager and restaurant manager all balanced their takings and delivered them to the office, while Eddie was closing huge grey shutters and locking strategic doors. Soon after six the Hall's public areas were secured for the night, the state rooms dim and silent, and Eddie went up to his flat at last, legs aching after a long day when he had hardly sat down since eight in the morning. Katie, his wife, had finished her stint as shop assistant off the Red Corridor and she, too, had climbed the stairs. They were looking forward to an evening out with their daughter, home from university.

In the administrator's flat I was completing my session of exercises to my aerobics video-tape. I had to do it after the Hall closed because our television was in the living room, which is situated over the entrance lobby, and there had been complaints of elephants overhead! I was, therefore, in the habit of exercising in late afternoon, then taking a shower before cooking dinner; by the time the meal was ready, around seven thirty, Chris was usually finished in the office. On a good day, anyway.

At seven o'clock on this particular evening he was sitting at his desk in that room over the Red Corridor, aware of the park spreading beyond his wide window, a mellow sun lowering in the west over a dark bank of woods, ruminating cows in pasture dotted by oaks and chestnuts and backed by a rise that hides the lake. Above that hidden lake, a touch of mist began to gather as the air temperature changed; the slight veiling of the landscape lent a soft, Impressionist texture which Chris admired now and then, glancing up from his work.

Then something alien obtruded into the picture. A double-take confirmed it. An aircraft! Coming in low over trees beyond the lake, it seemed to be heading straight for the office window . . .

Peering into misty, slanting sunlight, Chris couldn't at first make out the craft's exact distance, or its size: for a moment it looked as big as a 747! With visions of headlines telling of the demolishment of Felbrigg Hall, he leapt up and yelled in the general direction of our kitchen, 'There's an aeroplane coming! An aeroplane's landing! Mary—!'

Another look showed him the craft dipping even further, below the tops of the trees in the pasture. Now he could get the scale of it. To his relief, it wasn't a jumbo jet but a single-man microlight. Bucking and weaving, it touched down in the pasture and bounced across the grass, much to the amazement of the cows, who stopped chewing and turned their heads to watch it chunter to a stop in the middle of their field.

By that time I had reached the office and together we stared at the spectacle. Felbrigg had given us a lot of surprises in its time, but this was the first visit by an aviator.

'He must be in trouble,' Chris surmised. 'You stay here while I go and see what's wrong.'

I watched from the window, wonderingly. One thing about life at Felbrigg – it was never dull.

When Chris reached the craft, the pilot was out of it and looking at his engine, trying to discover what the problem was and whether he could fix it. The cows were interested, too. They had never had a chance to look at an aircraft so closely before. Being curious creatures, they ambled over and stood in a semi-circle, much like human spectators.

It turned out that the pilot, Dick Clegg, was taking part in a Great Microlight Air Rally, in which forty assorted craft had departed from Manchester at 12 noon on Saturday, aiming to visit as many of the fifteen designated sites as was possible between then and 4 p.m. on the following Monday, by which time they all had to touch down at Haverfordwest, in Wales, before returning to Manchester. Checkpoints ranged as widely as Wick in Scotland, Sandown in the Isle of Wight, Davidston in Cornwall, and, of course, Northrepps International Airport in north Norfolk.

Dick had been aiming for an overnight halt at Northrepps when he developed technical trouble. He was only a couple of miles from his destination, but when he realized he wasn't going to make it he looked around for a suitable open space and saw Felbrigg Park ahead, opening its grassy arms invitingly.

'I'll phone Northrepps Hall,' Chris decided when he heard Dick's problem. 'Come on in and have a drink and we'll sort this out for you. Only ... perhaps we'd better move your machine out of the field or the cows will be rubbing themselves against it.'

The two men manhandled the aircraft towards the corner of the field and out through the gate, its wings just managing to clear the gateposts. Chris remarked later that the microlight had been misnamed; it was micro*heavy* as far as he was concerned. Pushing it across a field had exhausted him.

They sat in the office while Chris got through to Northrepps Hall and the staff of the International Airport. (If you're out that way and want to visit the airport, look for a strip of grass alongside a field a few miles from Felbrigg!) Dick told us he had been in the air since early that morning without a stop. He hadn't had anything to eat or drink. He refused my offer of supper, but he did have a terrible thirst and downed several pints of squash and a large pot of tea as we chatted and waited for the Northrepps people. Dick was still hoping to get his craft airborne again before dark so he could add Northrepps to his tally for that day and set off fresh in the morning, but with every minute the evening mist was thickening and the sun sinking. It looked as though he might be grounded for the night.

Men soon arrived and sorted out whatever was wrong with the engine, but by that time the sun was almost gone and night would soon be drawing in. But Dick was eager to try to fly that last mile or two, so once again they trundled the machine back into the field and Chris and the other men stood watching as it bumped away, gathering speed, sending cows lumbering off in all directions. Finally it lifted into a graceful take-off and soared away, into the misty dusk, the sound of the engine slowly dwindling to silence.

We heard later that Dick had been the only one of forty competitors to check in at Northrepps. In fact, he went on to win the race, having called in at more checkpoints than any of the other thirty-eight who finished.

Another aerial visitor came one day when the Hall was closed. This time it was a helicopter and he was expected – Anglia Television were doing a feature on the great eighteenth-century landscape gardener Humphry Repton (1752–1818), who lived at Sustead near Felbrigg and became a friend of William Windham III. When, in 1792, Windham was appointed to the office of Chief Secretary to the Lord Lieutenant of Ireland, he took Repton, his friend and neighbour, as his private secretary. Long before the landscaper became famous, he is believed to have been responsible for some of the planting at Felbrigg, wonderful swathes of trees that now produce such a profusion of different greens in the spring, some with blossom, and one or two copper beeches as a dark contrast. The pinnacle of his achievement, however, was the creation of nearby Sheringham Park, which is being brought back to its former glory by the National Trust. For their programme, Anglia Television had asked permission to film in Felbrigg Park and had advised us of which day they would be coming.

Naturally we had talked about it to our staff and friends. What we didn't expect was that one of our regular visitors would bring along his family that day, all dressed up ready to be seen on the telly! All morning they hung around the front of the Hall, watching expectantly every vehicle that came through.

Finally we heard the helicopter and, seeing the Anglia logo on it, realized it was to be aerial filming. When they seemed to be coming very close to the house, Chris became a bit concerned that the downdraught might damage the masonry or slates. Thinking that the chopper was going to land in the park, he went dashing out to speak to the crew, but by the time he got to the front of the house they were sweeping past at a safe distance. He waved at them, trying to indicate that they shouldn't come too close, but they only circled before coming past once more, even further away, then melted into the distance.

'Probably just doing a recce run,' said Chris to the smartly dressed family. He had had ample experience of the media by then, so he was accustomed to their odd little ways. 'They'll probably come back and do a slow pass across the front here, if you'd like to wait.'

So the family waited. And waited. The Anglia helicopter had flown like the cuckoo in August, not to be seen again that year.

When eventually we saw the feature on Repton its main thread was about Sheringham, naturally enough. Sheringham Park was entirely Repton's vision and there still exists a Red Book of his designs for the park – another of the Trust's treasures. But the programme did show some shots of Felbrigg woods, and a view of the Hall from an unusual angle – high up in the air with the woods behind and a glimpse of sea in the distance. Those dots by the house might be the watching family, getting their moment of fame; but the only living creature evident on the video is the tiny, running figure of the administrator, frantically waving his arms.

'The black bat, night . . .'

Daytime visitors are, generally, welcome at Felbrigg. By night, however, we expect only those who have been invited.

One hot evening I was in our mezzanine living room with the television and lamps on when I became aware of another presence and saw the dark, flickering wings of a bat which had slipped in through the open window. On summer evenings bats swoop round the Hall by the dozen, a welcome addition to the Felbrigg family, but not quite so welcome indoors. I admit I cowered away when it sliced the air near my head; I watched it for a while, over the back of the sofa, hoping it would find its way out again, which eventually it did. Relieved, I ran and shut the window behind it.

Going to find Chris and tell him of our visitor, I discovered the main bedroom light on, with the huge sash window open, and a whole family of bats sailing round and round the central light. The bedroom is another room of stately proportions, with a very high ceiling – the previous administrator had his own four-poster bed in there – so the bats had lots of room to fly. They must have come in after the green, gauzy-winged flies which the light had attracted. Now they were zooming round and about, occasionally changing direction, dipping and swooping in dizzying aerial display. I hovered in the doorway, wincing every time one came too close, afraid that it might get past me and fly even deeper into the flat. When Chris came, however, he went to stand in the centre of the room and let the bats whisper round him. Not one of them touched him, though he felt the breath of their wings on his face. We counted thirteen of them.

One by one, as the supply of flies diminished, they found their way out via the wide-open window. But evidence of their passing remained – bat droppings everywhere, much like those of mice, with which we were well acquainted, except that these were not only on the bed, carpets and dresser but stuck, as I discovered in daylight, all over the upper parts of the walls – mute evidence of the power of centrifugal force. To this day I'm not absolutely sure I removed every one of those messages; I'm a bit short-sighted and some may have been too high up for me to see.

A National Trust by-law decrees that no one without authority may be anywhere on the estate between dusk and dawn. For the sake of security we have occasionally had to question people as to their purpose in being around the Hall and the park, or the woods, during those hours.

One such incident began late one summer night when we were up in our large sitting room, the grand one with the two huge bays facing east and south. The room is enormous, with a sixteen-foot-high ceiling; it was furnished mainly with spare pieces from the attics, but we had also acquired a very large three-piece suite (going cheap because no modern house had the room for it!), which still didn't manage to fill half the empty spaces. In winter the room was a barn, bitterly cold and used only on special occasions when we had heaters going for hours to get it comfortable. In summer, though, with its windows open to the evening breeze, standard lamps aglow and stars beginning to prick out in a royal blue sky, the room is a lovely place to be.

We were quietly enjoying a rare peaceful moment, listening to owls hoot and bats squeak while the cows in the pasture lowed softly to their calves, when a peculiar clanking sound, completely alien to that setting, came clearly through the open windows. We got up to look out, but with only the stars to light the park the night lay too dark for us to see much apart from the outlines of trees. The strange noise came again, from somewhere along the drive, a hundred or so yards away.

When Chris telephoned the police, they promised to send one of their officers through the park to have a look. Too concerned to leave it at that, Chris decided he had to investigate for himself. Off he went, equipped only with a trusty torch.

As he approached one of the field gateways, he saw a large vehicle parked there without lights, with its tail-gate down. Skirting round at a safe distance, he observed at least two figures near the van, one of them in the field where the cows and calves were moving restlessly, disturbed by their stealthy visitor.

The patrolling police car turned up just then and Chris flagged it down and told the constable what was happening. They drove up to the van and asked what was going on.

The intruders proved to be a local couple who were, apparently, known to the police. They said they had just come out to do a bit of courting. Having no evidence to prove otherwise, the police asked them to move on, which they did, leaving the estate with due haste.

As their tail-lights faded, Chris said, 'If they were out for a bit of courting, why did they have the tail-gate down?'

'Fresh air?' one of the policemen suggested.

'Question is,' said the other with a grin, 'why did they have to come out here at all? I happen to know they live together!'

We didn't hear of any cattle going missing, so maybe we were wrong. Or had our vigilance deterred potential rustlers? A farm a few miles away had some beasts stolen not long afterwards, so who knows?

Enchanted evening?

The lake, secluded in a hollow well away from the Hall, attracts its share of illicit night-time lingerers. Fishermen sometimes decide to camp there, or youngsters might use the site for a party, complete with beer cans by the score. Overnight visitors are a nuisance, especially when they leave their litter for someone else to clear up, and if it isn't beer cans or broken bottles it is often yards of fishing line, which can be dangerous to birds and animals. Once we had to call out the local swan rescue man when a swan got itself sadly tangled. Our unofficial bailiff, Ian, the local blacksmith who lives not far from the lake, usually asks people to leave if he discovers them there after dusk. Sometimes though, if he feels the problem may be too much for him to handle alone, he calls the Hall and reports lights, or voices, or drunken carousing or whatever.

Several times Chris answered a call from Ian and then went off down to the lake to investigate, leaving me to worry. 'Call the police if I'm not back in an hour,' was his usual cheery farewell. (The lake is a long walk away.)

After a spate of these calls, when neither he nor Ian had been able to catch whoever was fishing late and illegally (we had sold no tickets for that period), he decided to try another ploy: he would go down to the lake early and lie in wait for these people, who seemed to come around dusk. So he and I set out, suitably equipped in walking shoes and with a few sandwiches and a bottle of wine to keep us going while we waited.

It turned into one of the most enchanted evenings I can remember. As we arrived at the lake, sunset was flooding the sky with gold, lighting the water, but under the trees twilight was gathering. The lake is thickly wooded along one shore, with rustic benches to sit on. All was quiet and still that evening. Midges danced on the gilded water, fish plopped, waterbirds swam silently to and fro, the slightest breeze quivered in tender leaves, and a woodpecker began hammering. Then, to crown it all, we saw the vivid flash of a kingfisher.

We seemed to be miles away from everything, supping on sandwiches and wine as the dusk thickened and the sun went down. Ah, that was the life – the life that people imagined we had all the time. It did have its moments.

But our reason for being there – the trespassing fishermen – didn't appear that night. Soon it was dark under the trees though the sky above remained light with the first stars showing. And only then did we realize we had omitted to bring a torch – the sun had been shining when we left home.

Thinking of the long trek back across the fields, I said, 'Hadn't we better go before it gets too dark to see? They won't come now, surely?'

'They might be coming late to camp overnight and fish at dawn,' Chris said. 'If they are, they'll probably be coming soon. They'll park in the back lane – that's where Ian's seen their car. Let's go back that way. We might meet them.'

It meant putting a mile or so on to our journey, but . . . well, OK, if he thought it was necessary.

We left the lake, via a swampy meadow that seems to be wet even in the driest periods. It has a permanent walkway for visitors, but we left that official path and turned on to the fishermen's way, an overgrown track by the side of a stream and across a field thicketed with gorse bushes.

By this time it was really dark. I couldn't see where I was putting my feet, whether in cow-pats or thistles or merely quagmire, but I could just make out Chris's tall figure ahead, and beyond him the trees near the wall reared their outlines black against the washed blue and streaked orange candyfloss of the western sky. Then, to my horror, I made out other outlines – a herd of cows gathered round the gate.

'The bull's not with them, is he?' I hissed.

'Probably so. Yes, look, he's right by the gate.'

'Oh, thanks a lot,' said I, knowing my husband and his leg-pulling.

He wasn't joking. As I peered through the darkness I could see the massive shape of the bull with his white-patched face

The bull lifted his head and bellowed a warning . . .

turned towards me, staring, shifting uneasily. When he lifted his head and bellowed a warning, as if telling us to stay clear of his harem, I stopped.

'Just keep going,' Chris advised. 'Keep walking steadily. He'll move out of the way.'

I admired his confidence. The bull was showing signs of disliking our proximity and the cows around him were beginning to toss and leap away. He bellowed again (you can't call that bass threat mooing).

'Move yourself!' Chris ordered, waving his arms, making a lunge at the bull – between it and me, my hero! As the great chunk of mobile steak stamped a few paces backwards, I made it to the kissing gate and got through, with Chris a pace or so behind me. The bull stared after us, malevolent and menacing in the darkness.

'Told you he'd move,' said Chris smugly. 'You weren't scared, were you? He's a soft old thing, that bull. Wouldn't hurt a fly.'

Now he told me.

There was no sign of cars on the corner where fishermen usually park, nor were there any vehicles in the lane. We called in at Ian's cottage to let him know we had done a patrol and all seemed clear for that night at least, and then we made our way back to the Hall – by a different route, I'm pleased to say. I don't think I could have faced that bull again.

More menacing night callers came undetected another evening. Next day three visitors who had trekked across the field to the church, which now stands separate from both Hall and village, discovered signs of damage. The intruders had broken into some cupboards, and into the bell tower; they had also moved furniture, and three tombstones had been shifted, though whatever they had hoped to find they had been disappointed because there was nothing in the church worth stealing. Perhaps the worst aspect was that they had ruined the decorative white altar cloth by scrawling on it, apparently in brass-rubbing crayon, a message to the effect that 'I call to have a black Mass.'

No one took that hint very seriously. Our woodsman, Tom, who was also the church warden, was upset by the incident but concluded that it must have been a stupid prank by some local teenagers. He was particularly upset because only four years earlier, after previous vandalism, it had been decided to leave the church open rather than risk even worse damage by people trying to break in. Now that decision would have to be reconsidered.

As always when anything newsworthy happened at Felbrigg, the press wanted the administrator's reaction. By then we knew the local reporter fairly well; he was a frequent visitor, and he knew that Chris would provide him with a few quotes, so he came along and they had a chat.

'Mind you,' Chris said at one point, 'I don't think it can be true that they had a black Mass.'

'Why not?' asked Keith.

'Well, don't you need a virgin for a black Mass? I don't know where they'd find one of those round here . . . or anywhere in East Anglia, come to that.'

Keith laughed, and started to make notes.

'For heaven's sake!' Chris cried, realizing what he had said. 'Don't quote me on that. I'll be skinned alive.'

Fortunately, no hint of this bad joke hit the headlines.

Facilities for the less able

Early in 1989 we were delighted to be able to open a new lavatory block, which is now available to everyone visiting the park. Before then, the only public lavatories were deep in the house and to reach them visitors had either to be members or pay for entry. It was a great relief – to them and to us – when the spanking new block was opened, with spacious modern facilities including a room for the disabled and a nappy changing area.

Later that year, we were visited by Valerie Wenham, the Trust's Disabled Adviser, who brought with her a man named Slim Flegg, a volunteer who travelled the country for the National Trust. He had lost both his legs and, though he was pretty nippy on a pair of crutches, he was planning to explore Felbrigg from the comfort of one of our wheelchairs, with me as his pusher. Just to test facilities, you understand. Despite his name, Slim was a very large chap: it wasn't only the facilities he tested on our long tour round every one of Felbrigg's delights. He was a great character, full of fun, and we spent an enjoyable morning together.

First, I fetched one of our available wheelchairs, well inflated in the tyre area (I hoped). With Slim comfortably settled, we went to the main door and did the tour as most visitors do. The ticket desk first: Slim showed his membership card and was greeted in usual cheery fashion by Jose, our ticket seller. Then into the Great Hall – a vision of early Victorian bad taste, in my untutored opinion. It was redecorated in neo-Jacobean style in the 1840s by William Howe Windham, who added overdone spiky door-cases, a cornice of alternating 'Green Man' masks and fleurs-de-lis, and gave the ceiling huge bulbous pendants which resemble nothing so much as inverted whirls of soft ice cream. They look like solid plaster but are, in fact, wood painted white and may well have been intended to show off the then new skill of wood-turning by lathe. W. H. Windham also filled the upper portions of the windows with a colourful display of stained glass, some of it from St Peter Mancroft church in Norwich.

The Great Hall is the favourite haunt of a regular volunteer room warden named Owen. He has a lovely way of greeting visitors: 'Welcome to Felbrigg. If there's anything you can't tell from your guide book, do ask.' And then he stands back and waits to see whether anyone will require him to dip into his vast store of knowledge. He loves to talk about the Great Hall; he knows all about the stained glass and the bronzes, the portraits, the books, the décor ... Which titbit of erudition will be required today?

Owen tells the story of an afternoon when several visitors were in the room but he was aware of one man who evidently wanted to ask something but was a little shy. Slowly the man edged closer to the corner where Owen was standing, and Owen mentally flicked through his notes on the room. What was it the man wanted to know about? The Coromandel screen, perhaps, or the unfinished portrait of the late squire?

At last the man summoned the nerve to speak, nodding nervously at Owen. 'Afternoon. Mind if I ask a question?'

'Not at all.' Owen was expansive, longing to share his enthusiasm for the room. 'Anything I can help with, you've only to ask.'

'Then, can you tell me . . . where did you buy your tie?'

Beyond the Great Hall lies the Dining Room, painted a delicate, fading lilac, with a wonderful plaster ceiling and ornate rococo adornments on the walls framing family portraits and mirrors in pleasing symmetry. It is a much less cluttered room, the great polished table bearing a crystal candle-holder, the sideboards decked with delicate porcelain.

As Slim, Valerie and I continued our tour, the wheels of the chair whispered on the drugget which protects the carpets. I was giving Slim my potted version of the Hall tour since by then I had registered the most important facts about each room, though on detail our experienced guides left me looking like an amateur. We passed into the richly decorated Drawing Room with its rainbow-sparkling chandelier, its red silk walls and curtains, and much gilding on furniture and wall sconces. This décor is echoed again in the last room on the ground floor, the Cabinet, where the gentlemen would withdraw to smoke and talk about the things that gentlemen talked about – politics and art, we're led to believe. Were our ancestors really that earnest? Here is displayed the collection of art treasures that William Windham II brought back from his Grand Tour.

Next there's a long corridor with cabinets of glassware and porcelain on display, and as you head back towards the front of the house you come into the staircase hall, lit from high overhead by a great square lantern of a skylight. This, of course, is where a wheelchair has to stop, at present – though that didn't deter Chris when one chair-bound lady was particularly keen to see the first floor, where are the Library and the splendid guest bedrooms. Chris carried her up while her relatives brought her wheelchair, and he carried her down again when they had completed their tour. However, no way could I carry Slim; I was thankful when he said it wasn't necessary.

We 'escaped' via what's known as the Bird Corridor, a

passageway designed to give the servants access from the kitchen area to the Dining Room and the back stairs. This broad, stone-floored corridor, with its tall windows looking on to the rear garden, is decorated with cases of stuffed birds, shot and mounted in Victorian times. Some visitors might be distressed by the display, but it is the way our ancestors showed their trophies, and how children in those times learned about wildlife; so the birds are a valid historical lesson, if grisly to our more enlightened eyes.

Access by wheelchair to the Old Kitchen tearoom was, we discovered, relatively easy with wide doors and space under tables for the chair to fit. We enjoyed a cup of tea and Slim and Valerie told me of their visits to other properties and some of the problems they had found. The National Trust is trying to make all its houses and parks available to the less able visitor but in some cases problems may be insurmountable. At Felbrigg, for instance, there is nowhere that we could readily install a lift to the first floor without completely altering the house.

After taking tea, the disabled visitor follows the usual route, down the Red Corridor and out into the Rose Garden, beneath the waterfall of wisteria which graces the doorway, and past the yellow peonies. From there, we made across the front of the house to reach the garden gate, where the west lawn spread before us, with the Orangery on its rise against a backdrop of shrubs and trees.

The garden paths, we discovered, were heavy going in places where the shingle lay thick, and some of the slopes made me puff despite my regular sessions of aerobics. But I never tired of walking in the shade of tall trees, by rhododendron which I had been amazed to discover came in many different colours apart from the common pale purple. You may stroll among them in several directions, but eventually your way leads you under the huge pines of the American Garden and out across a pasture, alongside the donkeys' grazing field, past a twisted sweet chestnut of ancient lineage. One of its neighbours had to be felled not long ago and its rings disclosed that it had been growing at Felbrigg since the mid-seventeenth century when Charles I was beheaded.

As you approach the garden gate, you pass under the branches of an old apple tree, where Ursula, in *The Rainbow*, sat during one scene of the serial and where, later, the *Daily Telegraph* had me pose for some publicity stills.

The walled garden is a quiet, secret place of many unexpected vistas, actually three walled gardens connected by gateways and arches, containing flowers and herbs, shrubberies and vegetables, with espaliered fruit trees round the walls – apples, pears, figs and cherries – and, of course, greenhouses for rearing young plants, tender varieties and exotic fruits. The grapes are a bit tart for my taste, but the raspberries, gooseberries and redcurrants are luscious, and I could spend hours in the herb garden just breathing in all the fragrances. Here, too, you will find a lawn where grow the hawthorns of which we are very proud – one of the best collections in England, still there despite the attempts of one 'expert' to have them grubbed up and yet another time-consuming rose garden planted.

At one time, the vistas in the garden were enhanced by wrought-iron gates of which the only sign now is their hinges on tall brick gateposts as you pass from one garden into the next. It has long been our dedicated head gardener Ted's dream to replace those gates. Chris talked the project over with our land agent, who suggested we should start a special Gates Fund which in a short time had climbed to over fifteen hundred pounds. Sadly, the last we heard, the relevant committee had refused permission for the project to go ahead. Now that we're no longer on the staff we have no power to change their minds (not that we ever did have much influence!), though as members of the Trust we shall continue to enquire. It is still our hope that, before Ted retires, he will see garden gates where they ought to be.

On leaving the garden, visitors generally cross the pasture back to the car-park, but with Slim and his chair we found the going too rough; we had to retrace our steps back through the gardens and round the Hall on the regular shingled pathways. To discover such anomalies was one of the reasons why he and Valerie had come.

Lastly, we visited the new lavatory block, with its airy anteroom and its spacious facilities, an added charm being the gold-crest which had taken up position in the ornamental trees and was flitting about the entry quite happily, singing its sweet song.

'Excellent!' Slim decided. 'Best loos I've seen in a long time.'

Chris always tried to give our less able visitors special attention when he could. He gave one blind man a personally guided tour, allowing him to touch where other visitors were requested not to. In the Bird Corridor, he showed the visitor a headless marble statue which had somehow found its way to Felbrigg from a graveside in ancient Greece.

'It's lost its head,' Chris said, 'so we aren't sure whether it's a man or a woman.'

'Oh,' said the blind man with a big grin, fondling the statue's buxom outline, 'it's a woman all right!'

Other visitors looked askance, wondering what on earth was going on – they had no idea the man couldn't see.

We were also pleased to have a hand in providing the first Braille guide for Felbrigg. Our volunteer friend Sallie did a lot of work with talking books and knew an unsighted lady who possessed a Braille-writing machine. They suggested that they would be willing to produce a guide for us, if we could condense it to suitable length, so I offered to précis the short guide down to its essentials. Sallie passed that on, on tape, to her friend, and soon we were able to offer a Braille guide to anyone who needed one. I believe similar guides are now available at other properties.

Another elderly visitor, who refused to think of herself as disabled, made her slow way from the car-park with the aid of a stick, her family anxiously around her. She was nearly exhausted when she reached the entrance hall and had to sit down for a while to recover her breath.

Seeing the problem, and the family all hanging about in varying stages of impatience, Chris suggested a wheelchair for the tour of the house.

'Oh, Mother won't use a wheelchair!' her despairing daughter sighed. 'She refuses to accept that she has a problem. We've tried everything.'

What they hadn't tried was Chris's brand of persuasion. He

'Oh, it's a woman all right!' said
the man with a big grin.

sat and talked to the lady and explained how a chair would help her: she wouldn't get so tired; she wouldn't need to worry about holding up her family; what was more, she could sit back and look at the lovely ceilings as she went. Then, if she wished to climb the stairs, she might be rested enough to do that in slow stages, whereas if she tried to walk all the way she wouldn't have the strength to get to the first floor.

Funny how a stranger can often achieve what a family have tried for years to do. The lady agreed to try it. She toured the house – *and* she saw the gardens – from the comfort of her borrowed chair.

A year later, the same family party returned, with Mother already ensconced in a wheelchair this time. The daughter asked at the desk if she could speak to Chris. 'I don't know how you managed it,' she told him. 'But after we'd been here last year Mother suddenly seemed to realize what a boon a chair would be. She has her own now, and we've been all over the place on outings we couldn't have dreamed of before. It's made all our lives so much better. We can't thank you enough.'

Moments like that make it all worthwhile.

. . . bump in the night

Noises after dark can be disturbing when you live in a large, secluded old house. The normal sounds of the wind in the eaves, or the fabric creaking and groaning and settling with changes of temperature, like an old woman scratching and stretching, relieved to be rid of her corsets, had become familiar to us. But now and then unusual noises obliged us to investigate.

Late one summer evening, when Chris was watching the after-midnight replays of that day's Wimbledon matches, a terrific crash shook the house. It startled me out of bed and I went down to see what was happening. Had something fallen in the main Hall somewhere? Or had it been a window breaking – someone attempting a robbery? One consolation was that the alarms had not reacted, which probably meant that no one had got into the Hall – unless, of course, someone had already

95

interfered with the system. When you're responsible for a priceless property and its contents you can never be complacent.

'We'd better make a recce,' Chris said. 'We'll go round the Hall systematically.'

He didn't want to disturb Eddie and Katie unnecessariiy, not at that hour (it was nearly 1 a.m.) so we set out together, he unlocking doors while I stayed well back ready to run for a phone if something happened. Having established that each room in turn was clear of intruders, we shone our torches round looking for signs of anything that could have caused the crash – a fallen picture, perhaps. The noise had seemed quite close to the flat, but sounds can echo deceptively in that great house, so we checked everywhere.

There was nothing to be found. The crash remained a mystery. We reset the alarms and were beginning to climb the stairs to our flat when we detected a smell something like a four-ale saloon, or maybe it was a wine bar. Alcoholic fumes wafted up from the stairs below ours, which lead down into the cellar where Joan stores wine for the restaurant.

Unlocking the cellar door, we went down and at last discovered the source of the mystery noise: the crates of wine had not been stacked properly and two of them had crashed, smashing all their contents, leaving a dark stream slithering through the thick dust on the floor. Later, the cellar had to be sluiced out, but it scented our flat for some time.

Not long afterwards, a similar though less noisy crash had us investigating once again, this time without immediate result. But the next time Joan went down to the cellar she found that the ceiling over the stairs had collapsed in a welter of dust, cobwebs and ancient lath and plaster. I had wondered why our stairs were more draughty than usual, and where all the dust was coming from!

That *is* one of the drawbacks of living in these places: your private life is never really private; it all gets entwined with the Hall and the job. Once, one of the rooms near our flat had its floorboards taken up and its joists and woodwork thoroughly sprayed against dry rot, wet rot, and beetle. Which was all very well except that the space under the floor connected with the space under our sitting room, and for a fortnight the fumes were so strong that we couldn't sit in there without feeling sick. We still wonder what long-term effects those toxic fumes might have had on our health.

When alarms are being checked or updated, one's home is invaded by workmen banging and hammering, sometimes for weeks on end. Scaffolders peer in at the windows; painters go roaming, 'just wanting a look'. And there was the priceless time when our bedroom was fully lit all night every night by security lamps guarding the scaffolding outside, when the roof was being releaded. Not to mention that when you're sitting on the downstairs toilet you can hear every word being spoken in the Bird Corridor below . . .

However, we were more fortunate than friends at another property, whose quarters were divided by a corridor down which visitors had to walk when the house was open. This corridor separated the administrator's bedroom from his bathroom, and most of the time it was not a problem. However, the administrator's wife recalls the time when she was ill in bed with a gastric upset and was forced, in her dressing gown, to run the gauntlet of astonished onlookers every time she needed the bathroom. Not funny. Well, not at the time.

4

A sting in the tale

Plagues of insects seem to come and go in cycles – one summer it's ladybirds, another it's greenfly. One year we were especially plagued by wasps, starting when two of the National Trust Volunteers, working in the woods, had to be rushed to hospital after being badly stung. Many visitors complained of the nuisance the insects were making.

Our tenants, Gill and Henry, who live in The Retreat (the lovely mews house which the last squire modernized for his own comfort, off the grass courtyard at the back of the Hall), had discovered a wasps' nest in their roof space and asked the gardeners if they would attend to it. Ted and Mark were seen rolling away a wheelbarrow burdened with a vast off-white ball which must formerly have been the home of thousands of wasps.

Discovering that several other nests were burgeoning in various spots under Felbrigg's eaves, Chris sent for a pest control operative, who came, like the Daleks, prepared to Exterminate! But having examined the sites he was reluctant to use his toxic spray; he feared it would harm the house martins who were feasting on the buzzing, stinging menaces, evidently finding them quite a delicacy. 'You don't want to poison the birds,' the man said. 'Anyway, you know, wasps go hunting quite a distance from their own nests. The ones that are causing a problem round here aren't your own local wasps, so even if I did get rid of them you'd still have the problem. They're coming from somewhere else.'

Chris decided to leave the resident wasps and house martins to sort it out amongst themselves.

Soon a new chapter in the wasp saga opened, at the base camp over the old stables. This 'base camp' provides basic accommodation for parties who come to stay at Felbrigg – National Trust Volunteers coming to help us out with jobs in the woods, school or other youth groups, almost anyone, in fact, who cares to make use of the facilities. These comprise two dormitories at either end of the block with a central communal area for dining, showering and relaxing. The rooms lie over what was once part of the stables, and it was here that someone discovered yet another huge wasps' nest.

Despite the pest expert's reassuring words about the habits of wasps, to leave one so near the base camp looked uncaring of our visitors' safety, so Chris asked the gardeners if they could work their magic again and remove the nest. The base camp was occupied at the time by a school party, boys and girls aged between ten and twelve who had come with their teachers to spend a week with us and explore Norfolk from their base at Felbrigg. They, of course, thought the affair of the wasps a great adventure.

After their departure, some of them wrote thank you letters. One boy said that he had enjoyed his stay at Felbrigg very much. He had liked sleeping in the dormitory and exploring the woods, and watching them remove the wasps' nest had been ace! It was just a pity that there hadn't been any television provided: he had had to miss *Home and Away* and *Neighbours*. 'Still,' he concluded philosophically, 'you can't have everything.'

New building work

The base camp was slightly altered during the building of the new Park Restaurant. The Victorian stable block had been used until then as garages for our cars. The new restaurant took over the garages *and* the old base campers' games room, while its new water tanks took up space in one of the dormitories above. The cars had to be parked outside as builders began to change the inner face of the 165-year-old stables in order to create a spacious new restaurant.

As I recall, the worst bone of contention was the flooring:

experts insisted that, since it had once been a stable, the only possible authentic material was extremely expensive York stone. Joan argued that, since it was now to be a restaurant, she would prefer something more level and less likely to accumulate dirt. The experts, however, had their way. In consequence, the restaurant floor is nigh impossible to keep clean, and the wobbling tables have to be adjusted by sticking bits of card under their legs. 'Nuff said.

The building work and its attendant problems continued all through the summer, while thousand after thousand of visitors passed through. Chris could have spent his afternoons in the office, but he preferred to be a visible force about the house, ready to help wherever he was needed. Eddie, Joan and Heather, the new shop manager, all knew they could turn to him at a moment's notice, while the volunteers looked forward to the few minutes he tried to spend with each of them every day. His regular presence became a unifying force, blending each separate area into part of the team. Because of it, the staff felt secure, able to get on with their own jobs while knowing there was a safety net should something happen that they couldn't cope with – at least, that's what Chris hoped and believed was happening. Certainly that was his intention.

Fresh light on old stories

Occasionally, members and friends of the Trust donate items of interest to be kept for the nation, things which may be relevant to Felbrigg and which family and friends may disregard, or be tempted to sell without taking into account their local interest. One such item is a book, in itself of little importance, an ordinary hardback with gilded edges. Its uniqueness lies in that when the fore-edges of the pages are slightly spread, they reveal, painted on them, a miniature copy of a picture by Humphry Repton, the landscape gardener mentioned earlier. His original drawing shows Felbrigg Park and lake with the Hall in the distance, a carriage, and three men planting trees – which have now grown tall, so that this particular view is no longer possible. However, someone took the trouble to copy it in wonderful detail on to the page-edges of this book. You could handle it, even read every page, without ever suspecting what lies hidden there.

Sad, 'Mad' Windham

Another unexpected sidelight on one of Felbrigg's tales turned up one day when a gentleman brought in a copy of an old railway notice, dating from the 1860s. It sternly forbade all railway employees to allow 'Mr W. F. Windham' to have any part in any function whatsoever to do with the railway. He was not to blow the whistle, open or close doors, interfere with passengers or act as a guard. Any member of the railway staff who allowed Mr Windham to perform any semi-official duty upon railway premises was threatened with instant dismissal.

This notice refers to William Frederick Windham, the unfortunate scion of the family who in the 1860s was the subject of a sanity trial which filled acres of newsprint. Indeed, when Chris and I consulted the newspaper archives we discovered that the reports of the trial took up far more column inches than the Prince Consort's last illness.

The jury eventually found young Windham capable of managing his own affairs, but as the *Daily Telegraph* said at the time,

> The verdict . . . is not a hesitating one; it pronounces him sane and competent; and in doing so in face of the immense mass of evidence collected to prove him fool, liar, brute, and prodigal, it simply asserts that these are disgraceful names, but not the names of madness.

Harsh words, but evidently not undeserved. Two years later the estate had to be liquidated to clear the young squire's debts. After that, Wm. F. spent a few years driving a mail coach, playing at being a guard on the railway, and generally making a buffoon of himself in the area. Hence the railway notice, which added yet more documentary evidence to the store we had already garnered.

'Mad' Windham's story is well documented elsewhere, but we came across some old newspaper cuttings that added a few more morsels of interest. For instance, the *Daily News* for 8 March 1862 (soon after the trial) says:

> Mr Windham, so well known in connexion with a recent enquiry, has been amusing some of the Windsor folks for several days past with his freaks, by liberally dispensing his hospitality at various public-houses in the shape of champagne, spirits, beer, steaks, etc., to cabmen, soldiers, and cads.

Cads, by heaven! Reading between the lines of the evidence, it appears that William Frederick was perhaps what would today be termed 'educationally disadvantaged', or perhaps simply, as one of his contemporaries said, 'a damned young spendthrift and fool'.

On one journey, with his coach careering wildly down a green lane, he ran his horses into a pedestrian and broke both of the man's legs. Another cutting, from 1865, reveals that:

> Mr W. F. Windham, while driving his coach a short time ago, ran into an omnibus which plies between Norwich and Cromer, and an action was brought against his employer, the owner of the coach, for damages to the amount of £8 11s, which, with a small deduction, the Judge of the County Court awarded. In the course of the case it transpired that Mr Windham receives £1 per week as driver of the coach. In 1861 he had £5000 to £6000 per annum from his estates [A substantial fortune in those days].

Saddest of all is the afterword we found in a gossip column of 19 November 1898, which recalls the long-gone days of the coaching inns, many of which went out of business with the coming of the railways. The writer makes special mention of the Norfolk Hotel in Norwich, which, he says,

> ... is doomed to disappear within a very short period ...
> With the Norfolk, old citizens will ever associate THE NAME OF DURRANT ... When White's first Norfolk directory came out in 1836, there was a Durrant in possession. Dan of that ilk was a famous whip of forty years

ago. In the memories of that time, or a little later, the most prominent figure at the Norfolk was that of William Frederick Windham – 'Mad Windham' as they called him – who drove the Cromer coach, first as a plaything, and at last for a livelihood when the fortune he inherited had been dissipated ... His shambling, uncouth figure was well known in the streets of Norwich in the early sixties, and he obtained something like a national fame after THE FAMOUS CASE in the Court of Exchequer at Westminster at the end of 1861 ...

We may safely say that the loss of THE FELBRIGG DEMESNE was the consequence of the issue of this enquiry, while the spendthrift sank lower and lower in the social scale, till he was reduced to the level of those with whom he had in earlier days elected to associate. Of his marriage and all that came of it this is not the place to speak. It will be enough for us to draw the curtain with William Frederick Windham's death in the February of 1866 in the little bedroom at the hotel, up the leaded staircase past the bar. It was said that in the last few weeks the man who had squandered thousands had not the wherewithal to buy a meal, and when the end had come there was no one to order a coffin for him, and a shirt of dead Dan Durrant's had to be put upon him in default of one of his own.

That last sentence brings a lump to my throat. What a sad end for the bright little boy, known in the family as 'Gla', whose portrait hangs above the door of the Morning Room at Felbrigg. There he stands, his long white, lace-trimmed knickers showing under his blue-skirted coat, with his fair hair neatly combed: the only son and heir of a great Norfolk family, destined to be buried with 'dead Dan Durrant's' shirt as a shroud.

When he died, he was just twenty-five years old.

Little darlings

The vast majority of our visitors are a treat to meet. Most of them, from the 'ordinary' family to the genuine aristocracy, are friendly and interested. Children, too, can be a delight, so interested and eager, and Chris always enjoyed the chance to take a school party round. But it is difficult to enjoy the company of certain young persons whose passing is like the proverbial hurricane. Rope stanchions go down like ninepins; the peace is disrupted by shouts of temper; sticky, dirty fingers leave marks on silk fabrics and wallpapers, or flick light switches. Consternation follows such a family all round the house; the room wardens try to conceal their exasperation, but it is not always possible.

One small tornado passing through, committing all kinds of mayhem and totally unrestrained by its parents, had the misfortune to come up against one of our lady guides of the old school. She stopped the child from kicking a glass panel in a bookcase, and soundly reprimanded him for being a naughty boy. His mother turned on her, ready for battle.

'Oh, but isn't he a beautiful child!' our volunteer purred. 'Such a lovely little face!' The flattery completely stalled the irate mother.

Our guides have a wonderful way with visitors, using their individual skills to draw out questions and add to the interest of the visit. But they do feel protective of Felbrigg and any hint of risk to the house or its contents makes them rear up defensively. I remember the outrage that rippled through the Hall when a lady in a motorized wheelchair sailed through. It wasn't the chair they minded, or the three children who raced about sliding on wooden floors and generally behaving as though they were in a playground. No, it was the fact that under the lady's chair a large wire basket, presumably intended for shopping, was crammed with fresh blooms and foliage torn from our rhododendrons and azaleas. Guide after guide reported it, but we were powerless to do anything about it. What can you say to someone like that?

'Making water'

Katie and I watched from an upper window of the Hall as great fire engines and tenders rolled up one after another. Our husbands waited to greet them and open the field gate, so that three of the tenders could space themselves across the pasture, their intention being to test the logistics of pumping water directly from the lake to the Hall, should mains water prove insufficient. No, Felbrigg was not on fire, I'm pleased to say. We were watching a brigade exercise – a necessary precaution.

'Pugh, Pugh, Barney McGrew . . .' Katie and I couldn't help recalling the little firemen of television's *Camberwick Green* as the uniformed officers hurried about, unrolling and connecting hoses all the way across the field to disappear over the distant rise. We could see they were having problems of some kind, but at last the connections all seemed to be ready and ladders were raised up to the roof above us. A squad of firemen climbed up with their hoses and soon great arcs of spray were cascading out from the roof over the courtyard and the grass beyond. Chris and Eddie ran for dry ground.

In such cases, the hoses 'make water', as they call it, off the roof rather than on to it, in case the pressure should damage slates or brickwork. If there were to be a fire, of course, water damage would be a secondary consideration.

Later, we all got together for a beer and a discussion of the problems they had encountered. At least we now knew that if we needed the fire brigade they were well prepared and acquainted with Felbrigg's eccentricities.

Fire – and the least chance of a risk of it – is something we take very seriously, especially after the example of poor tragic Uppark, the Trust house gutted by fire in 1989, and more recently Windsor Castle. Nowhere is safe. We must all be vigilant. If we forbid naked flames, and stop people smoking (especially workmen in sensitive areas), please bear with us.

More night alarums

On a hot August night, we were sound asleep in our vast, airy bedroom when we heard the doorbell ringing insistently. It was 1.30 a.m., as we discovered when Chris groped blearily for the alarm clock. He grabbed his dressing gown and went down to the grass courtyard door, where he found two or three of the

National Trust Volunteers in a panic. One of their number had fallen out of a window in the base camp.

Delaying only long enough to call up and tell me to phone for an ambulance, Chris went out to see what he could do. He is a trained Red Cross first-aider, thanks to a course he did soon after joining the Trust. Naturally, after phoning 999, I got dressed and went out myself – it's hard to stay aloof when these things happen on your doorstep.

The young man was lying on the far side of the stable block, where he had fallen from an upper window perhaps sixteen feet off the ground. He was unconscious, but Chris had got him comfortable and the others had brought blankets to cover him. Luckily the night was warm and the grass dry, but there was still the danger of shock.

We couldn't understand what had happened and neither could the Volunteers. They are responsible people, not yahoos. They had been out for a drink, but Tony hadn't had much; they had walked back and sat chatting for a while before going to bed in the dormitory bunks. Most of them were asleep when they suddenly heard a cry and, on investigating, had seen Tony lying outside on the grass below the window. Nobody knew how he had got there. The window had been on the latch to let in some air, but it was four feet from the dormitory floor. To get out of it, Tony must have climbed on to the bench seat and piles of rucksacks and belongings which stood under the window, opened the pane wide, and . . . Whatever had happened, he was in distress and we were concerned about him. The wait for the ambulance seemed interminable but at last the flashing blue beacon appeared in the distance.

Once Tony was safely on his way to hospital, we thought of his family. Someone had his home address and phone number, but there was no reply when we tried it. We waited until we heard from the hospital that he was 'comfortable' and then we phoned again. His family seemed to be away so we decided to leave it until the morning, when we learned that they had just returned from a holiday in France. They were travel-weary, hardly able to take in our news, but they said they would come at once, all the way from Liverpool.

It was late afternoon by the time they reached the hospital, to find Tony still too groggy to remember what had happened. His parents and young sister came to Felbrigg to hear the story from his friends. They asked if we could suggest somewhere they might stay for the night. What else could we do but offer our large spare Brown Room, which had a double bed and a single, just right for them? We hadn't anticipated becoming a B & B establishment, but they were welcome – it was just another of the unexpected roles one is called to assume when working for the National Trust.

The family were upset and disoriented by all the trauma on top of two long journeys. We gave them supper and sat talking, and next day after visiting Tony again they went back to Liverpool. Shortly afterwards, Tony was transferred to a hospital nearer home and in due course his parents let us know he was recovering.

The cause of the accident remained a mystery. I recall someone speculating that Tony might have been sleep-walking, but Chris and I never learned any more details.

Husky and Starch

Having had several problems with night-time trespassers – those elusive fishermen, the possible cattle-rustlers, and the black Mass incident, plus the time when we saw lights in the field after midnight, heard shooting, and discovered a chap out with a torch and a rifle after rabbit – and bearing in mind that access is strictly limited between dusk and dawn – we became extra vigilant on the estate after dark. One evening, coming home late under a brilliant moon, we saw two cars parked in a corner of the car-park, by the gate to the church field. Chris turned off the drive and we bumped slowly across the uneven grass, with our headlights full on to illuminate the other vehicles and warn the occupants of our presence in case they needed to comb their hair or something before we came too close. We couldn't see anyone inside, but you never know with courting couples.

No movement showed inside the cars, even when we stopped with our lights bathing them in halogen brightness. But we noticed lights jigging from the direction of the church, hand-torches, with several figures moving behind them.

'You take the car numbers,' Chris instructed me. 'I'll find out what they're up to.'

'Well, be careful!' said I, more out of habit than hope. His own health and safety came a sorry second when something threatened Felbrigg.

On this occasion the after-hours visitors offered no threat. They were a group of youths and girls, late teens and early twenties, wearing the sort of felt hats, ragged jeans and sloppy ponchos that people of that age like to wear. They said they were just out for a late stroll.

'You're not supposed to be on the estate after dark,' Chris explained. 'I'd be grateful if you'd leave.'

'Sure. We'll do that. We were going anyway.'

Chris came back to the car and we sat waiting until both of the other vehicles had moved off, heading for the gate a mile away. Though he couldn't say why, Chris had an uneasy feeling that something odd had been going on. When we reached the flat, he phoned the police and gave them the car numbers, just in case we should wake in the morning and find some calamity had occurred.

We were settling down in our living room with a hot drink and a last half-hour of late-night television when we saw more lights flash across our window, which we often left uncurtained. A car was pulling up outside the front railing, its lights shining across the shingle courtyard.

'If that's those youngsters back . . .' Chris opened the window and leaned out. 'Who's there?'

The visitor was a policeman in a patrol car, one of those with a silver-blue flash down the side. He had had the message about the intruders and had decided to come and check that all was well. Grateful for the prompt response, rather than shouting across the distance of the courtyard Chris went down to chat with the officer and tell him exactly what had happened. It worried him that the group had appeared to be coming from the church, especially in view of the vandalism not so long before.

'Shall we go and check the church?' the constable asked. 'We can go in my car.'

As Chris climbed in, the policeman beside him exclaimed, 'There's a vehicle coming!' He had seen the lights far off at the end of the car-park. 'Hang on, we'll find out what they're up to.' He backed up smartly, turning ready to meet the other vehicle, but it was driving round in a swift circle, to head away at speed towards the Cromer Gate. Its headlights, or perhaps the moonlight, must have shown up the fluorescent strip of the police car as it moved.

The policeman gave chase. Chris remembers it as 'white-knuckle, cops and robbers stuff'. On a single-track driveway with dodgy bends, they hurtled over clanging cattle-grids and between narrow gateposts, throwing up dust and stones as they slid round corners. The other car's lights had vanished. There was no sign of it along the drive, nor all the way under a tunnel of oak branches to the main gate. There the police car stopped, the driver turned off the engine and they listened.

Nothing. Perhaps the car had shot off along one of the trackways into the woods and stopped there, lights off, in hiding. If so, it had gone so far among the trees that they saw no hint of it as they slowly made their way back up the drive, peering down the dark openings among the oaks and rhododendron that lined the driveway.

The car had vanished.

They resumed their journey to the church, but not until they reached the car-park field did Chris and the constable see yet more lights coming along a farm track beyond the church, on a course which would bring the vehicle to the main drive about a hundred yards away. Was it the same car, trying to sneak away? The policeman killed his own lights as he turned his car to intercept; they hoped that this time the moonlight wouldn't give them away.

Slowly, stealthily (with Chris hardly breathing), the patrol car slid down the slight incline to converge with the route the other car must take as it moved along the bumpy track to join the drive. Its driver appeared unaware that he was being stalked.

As he turned on to the drive, heading for the Cromer Gate, the patrol car nosed in only feet behind him.

All at once, the officer switched on his headlights, his flashing blue beacon *and* his wailing siren. The occupants of the car in front must have had the fright of their lives. The car slewed on to the verge, off again, skidding and sliding until it came to a halt and the white-faced driver leapt out to confront his fate . . .

Poor man. He was a local photographer, whom Chris knew. He and his companion had come to take pictures of the lake by moonlight – a lovely thought, but they ought to have asked permission and informed us they would be there. Having been advised about the by-law and its restrictions on movements after dark, the pair drove off.

Finally, the policeman and his temporary partner made it to the church, which stood silent amid its shadows under the moon. Round by the gravel path, they approached the darkened porch, unlatched the wire mesh door . . .

'Do you want to go first?' Chris asked the officer, who had a torch in his hand.

'No, after you.' Such olde worlde politeness!

So Chris lifted the latch and pushed open the creaking church door. All was quiet. He turned his torchlight on ugly grey box pews and black-edged arms on the walls. Nothing appeared to have been disturbed.

We guessed that the earlier visitors might have been after 'magic mushrooms', the hallucinogenic fungi that grow in certain areas of our pasture and which had caused us problems before. But we never did find out what had happened to that speeding car.

Strolling in the park

The long light evenings of summertime entice many people to Felbrigg Park, to walk the woods and the lakeside, with or without their dogs, or to drive slowly through, admiring the views. We have often watched them from our windows, or from the cool heights of the roof parapet. Families come to play games; artists and photographers record the Hall in its various guises as the light changes and the seasons turn; some just like to sit in their cars and watch whatever might be going on. Ramblers ramble by, botanists study grasses, other groups enjoy a stroll. And as twilight falls lovers have been observed making imaginative use of picnic tables.

Bird-watchers often visit the park, too. One day great excitement swirled as twitchers with long lenses arrived by the carload and gathered by the fence, sights trained on something we couldn't see. 'It's a ring ousel,' we were told when we asked. Well, they seemed to be highly diverted by it, anyway, though it seemed odd to us that most of them came, saw, marked their sheet and went away without lingering to enjoy the sight of the rare bird. Much like train-spotting – even the anoraks were the same.

There came an evening when a long crocodile of children straggled through, with a couple of adults at their head. Chris was up in our big sitting room, listening to music as he did whenever he had the chance, while I was busy at the word processor in my tiny study – I find the evenings most conducive to writing, not so liable to interruption.

As you may have gathered, my husband has a mischievous sense of humour. That evening, seeing the approaching children, he decided to give them a treat. He fetched a sheet from the airing cupboard and, as the youngsters stood staring at the house, lagging behind their adult leader, Chris draped the sheet over himself and did a ghost-walk across the large front bay, moving out from one curtain and gliding behind the other.

Hidden by long forest-green velvet draperies, he peeped out to see what result his theatricals had had.

The children were animated now, pointing at the house, jumping up and down, clutching one another in both fright and glee, and calling their leader. Chris couldn't hear what they were saying, but the gist was clear enough: 'There was a ghost! We saw a ghost!'

The leader stared up at the house. Nothing there now. You must have been seeing things. Or are you having me on? Come on, stop being so silly, let's get on with our walk. There's no such thing as ghosts.

'Stop being so silly! There's no such thing as ghosts.'

The crocodile slithered back on its course, but a few curious and excited souls remained, still watching the window. So Chris did his undulating dance in reverse, and watched again as fresh animation ensued. This time the leader was impatient with all the nonsense. He rounded up the strays and off they all went, not without the odd wary backward glance. A few of them will forever be convinced that they saw a ghost at Felbrigg. Sorry, kids.

Felbrigg does, however, have one or two 'real' ghost stories. The Library is reputed to be haunted by the ghost of William Windham III who was once seen sitting in one of the green leather armchairs, so the story goes. Sensitive folk among our room guides and visitors have been known to say that they can feel an 'atmosphere' in the Library. Others detect no sign at all of any astral disturbance. One of our volunteers reports that one day, during a slight altercation with another guide, she heard children's voices in the attics above and saw beside her a figure that vanished. She later identified this figure as a lady in one of the photographs of long-ago Felbrigg.

Chris is a total sceptic and remains convinced that ghosts are 'all in the mind'. However, even he has his odd moments. In the woods one evening, at twilight, he saw what appeared to be the figure of a lady dressed all in shimmering white, with a veil over her head and face, like a bride. Anyone at all susceptible might have turned in another direction and hastened off to tell a convincing ghost story. Not Chris. He walked on, towards the figure, until he could see that the 'bride' was a growth of luminescent fungus on an old tree.

Could that be similar to what Dolly, one of the cleaners, saw one day when she was in the woods? She swears she saw a woman walking towards her, some distance away, on an undulating path whose turns and bumps would eventually cause the two to pass each other. The figure disappeared behind a dip in the ground, but when Dolly reached the next rise there was nothing to be seen. Ghost? Imagination? Trick of the light?

I like to keep an open mind on the subject, though I should love to be granted confirmation, one way or another. I, too, find the woods at twilight a bit disturbing – I find myself wincing out of the way of branches that are several feet away, or walking into twigs that seem not to be that close. But most of the time at Felbrigg I didn't feel nervous at all, even going round the old house in the dark when closing up late at night.

Another area which is supposed to be haunted is a little 'dressing room' in the administrator's flat. We called that tiny dressing room our 'Red Room' because I had fitted it with red curtains to go with the red carpet. Though it was just large enough for a double bed and bedside cupboards, it had drawers and shelves under the window, and an anteroom with a built-in wardrobe and a chest of drawers, so it formed a private little suite for guests. In the anteroom, a locked door connected with the Book Room, where the last squire's books and pictures are kept, together with display cabinets for people to see some of the interesting writings we have in our collection.

Rumours about the haunting of this area were so vague that we seldom spoke about them, certainly not to guests who were going to be sleeping there. I slept in the Red Room myself for a week, when Chris was ill, and found it cosier than our enormous main bedroom. However, one morning I happened to go into the anteroom of the suite before breakfast and, to my surprise, discovered the connecting door ajar. Normally, all such doors are checked, and shutters closed, as part of the daily close-down routine. Opening them breaks an electric circuit and sets off the alarms – or should do. But this one was an inch or two open and beyond it stretched the dark, cold spaces of the shuttered Book Room.

Hearing Chris about, I called to him, 'Have you turned the alarms off yet?'

'Just going,' he answered, disappearing down the stairs before I could say more.

Later, we argued about the details of it. *He* says I'm remembering it wrongly, that the door must have sprung open just after he switched off the alarms. I'm not so sure. Why would the door have sprung suddenly open? How did it come to be unbolted anyway? Ghosts? Or a forgetful human being? (Unlikely, but not impossible.) I'm still convinced that I found the door ajar *before* the alarms were deactivated. So why didn't they sound when the circuit was broken?

Good question.

Happy hippies

Our colleagues eleven miles away at Blickling Hall held a grand Fiftieth Birthday Party to celebrate Blickling's half-century as a property of the National Trust. On three evenings in July, the lovely gardens and grounds of the Hall were given over to hundreds of picnickers, many of them in fancy dress. There was music and dancing, a Radio Norfolk tent relaying nostalgic big-band sounds, food and drink stalls, a costume parade depicting fashions from the last fifty years, and at the end of each evening everyone gathered by the lake for a session of street-party songs which preceded the climax, in gathering twilight – of a spectacular firework display over the lake.

It promised to be too colourful an occasion to miss. We decided to buy tickets and go along in a party which included Joan and her assistant Eileen, with their husbands and some friends. Ten of us in all. We would take along some food, and a few bottles of wine. Next problem was what to wear. The idea was for people to go along in costumes from the forties onwards, which gave a vast choice from wartime to the nineties. The more daring could really have fun.

Taking into account items we already possessed, Chris and I elected to go as hippies. Cheap wigs are easy to come by – I had a long blond one and Chris a long black one, with a drooping black moustache. He hired an outfit of flared velvet pants and caftan, while I settled for an old Indian print dress from the back of my wardrobe, with a long underskirt to show beneath it. Both of us wore sandals on bare feet, loads of beads, feathers and flowers; we painted flowers and peace symbols on our faces, and wore dark glasses – mine were tiny granny glasses, which meant I had to leave off my own specs, so I was half blind. As a final touch, I carried a big basket laden with flowers amongst which we hid a bottle of wine and two glasses. And, thus attired, we walked the mile to the main gate of Felbrigg, where

Joan had arranged to pick us up – she was driving us all in a minibus.

Not until a passing car nearly went into a tree at the sight of us did we realize how strange we must look, two middle-aged hippies loitering at the gates of Felbrigg Hall. Joan and the others drew up, howling with laughter. They were in various guises – wide-boys in dark shirts and white ties, one of the women in a fifties suit and hat, a glamorous French maid (with an overcoat which she wore all night, too shy to take it off!).

Cars by the score queued to get into the vast car-park. Ladies in long evening dresses; soldiers and sailors; top hats and tail coats; blazers and boaters; American airmen ... Most people had settled for something not too outrageous, men in their own clothes with a straw hat, women vaguely fifties or sixties, with wraps. But a fair sprinkling had, like us, really gone to town and dressed up. There were even a couple of other hippies.

On that balmy evening, with the sun still shining, hundreds had gathered, wandering around the various stalls and attractions, listening to the music, or sitting in parties on the lawns and under the trees with their picnics, some very casual, others with chairs and tables all set out. The fancy dress greatly added to the colourful occasion.

Perhaps it was the wine we had drunk before we set out, or the wine we drank as we walked around the gardens, or perhaps it was the fact that no one knew us (even some people who knew us well didn't recognize us, though in a few cases Chris's voice gave him away); whatever the case, we weren't just dressed as hippies, we *became* hippies, wandering around with our basket of flowers, giving away blooms as we went, making the Churchill peace sign and wishing everyone 'Peace and love, brothers and sisters. Peace and love.' Some laughed, some wished us 'Peace and love' in return, some looked askance. Some even avoided us! Others wanted to take our photograph – we lost count of the number of snaps that we posed for, including some by the official photographer.

Around the VIP tent, notables stood in groups with their wine, some in Ascot dress, others in their usual evening mufti. Boring. I spied our historic buildings representative making his way through the crowd and went up to him, offering him a flower. 'Peace and love, brother John! Peace and love!'

'Oh . . . not now, not now.' He brushed me aside, embarrassed half to death at being accosted by this strange person. Next time we met, as our usual selves, he said he hadn't realized who I was. A fine excuse.

We encountered our regional director, handsome in a boater and striped blazer. 'Trust you two,' was more or less what he said, with a big grin. I'm still not sure he entirely approved.

Under some trees, a large party sat round a table laden with picnic victuals and wine bottles. At its head was one of our old friends, a regular visitor to Felbrigg and a supporter of many of our concerts and events. We had told him a few days before that we should see him at the party. As we approached, his friends laughed and accepted our greetings and after a moment of dumbfoundedness Stanley recognized us and leapt to his feet, gesturing at this pair of disreputable hippies and saying to his friends, with his customary good manners, 'May I introduce the administrator of Felbrigg Hall and his wife?'

In another part of the garden the costume parade had started, with a rather earnest master of ceremonies introducing the models in carefully chosen dress to represent the different eras of the fifty years. They were parading up the stone steps and along the parterre, some of them rather self-conscious. Among them was a group of rather well-dressed, well-groomed hippies. We joined them, adding an unexpected dimension to the parade as we displayed our full-blown scruffy-hippie costumes among the more respectable fashions. Still, the MC took it in his stride.

As we lined up along the terrace with the others, Chris found himself next to a young man he seemed to recognize, though he couldn't think where from. 'How did you get roped into this?' he asked.

'Oh, I'm, er, in a group that's staying at Felbrigg base camp. A few of us were asked to help out in this parade. What about you?'

So Chris had to confess his identity. They had met when the group booked in, though it was hardly surprising that the young man didn't remember.

After that, all that remained for us was to go to the VIP tent where they were having supper, and distribute yet more flowers and good wishes of peace and happiness. I was glad I wasn't wearing my glasses – I felt more incognito moving in a comforting blur.

It was a memorable evening. The singing at the end, the old Cockney and wartime songs, and then the fireworks! Shooting and sparking and exploding for what seemed ages, lighting up the night sky for miles. What a party! But that hippie couple had a lot to answer for, whoever they were.

A month later, the *Norfolk Magazine* published a page on which it showed photographs of the Queen Mother at Sandringham and the Princess Royal at the County Show; alongside is an account of the Blickling birthday party, illustrated with another photo – of a pair of middle-aged hippies in dark glasses, carrying a basket of flowers and making the V-sign of peace and love.

A cherished memory

The closest remaining relative of the last squire is his cousin, Colonel Dick Spencer. We had heard of Colonel Spencer, even corresponded with him, and Chris had said that we hoped one day to have the pleasure of meeting him. He had spent much time at Felbrigg when his cousin was alive, and had even helped Mr Ketton-Cremer to arrange the rooms as he wished them to be presented. In fact, had it not been financially impossible, Colonel Spencer might have inherited the house. As it was, he had not been back since the squire died, twenty years before.

Now, however, seeming encouraged by Chris's assurances of a warm welcome, the Colonel wrote that he and his wife would like to come. They chose a time and date when the Hall was open, and Chris left his diary clear for that afternoon.

Over the years we met many people who had known the squire. His old butler, Mr Ward, visited at the age of ninety; one-time maids brought memories of the past; other ladies had come picnicking as small girls when the squire held open house; and friends of his, and distant relatives arrived. All of them had stories to tell.

'May I introduce you to the Administrator of
Felbrigg Hall and his wife . . . ?'

Colonel Spencer's memories were especially interesting. He talked about the days he and his cousin had spent together at Felbrigg. Chris walked with him round the house and they discussed the different rooms and met all the guides who were on duty that day; then they came round the flat, which had once been part of the squire's private quarters. In his youth, Colonel Spencer had known 'Old Ketton' (Robert Ketton), who had lived in reclusive style in the room we used as a living and dining room. Our downstairs toilet had once been a bathroom, and our kitchen a linen room. His memories gave us new insight into the ways the flat and other areas had been altered over the years.

Before he left, Colonel Spencer was kind enough to say that he was delighted, and relieved, to have seen Felbrigg again. He had been reluctant to visit before, fearing what the Trust might have done to a house he loved. But it was all just as he remembered, just as his cousin had visualized it. Now he could go away reassured that it was being cared for in the right way.

That's a memory we especially cherish, though the accolade wasn't for us personally; we were just carrying on a tradition which, we hope, will continue for a long time.

Summer concerts

From April to October, on the first Friday of each month when the Hall is open, there is usually an evening concert in the Morning Room. When Chris took over, he elected to organize these concerts himself, to book the artists and advise them on their programme. Having seen three years of concerts of varying success, he had developed a good sense of what would be suitable and what would not. Many of our audience were regulars, fast becoming friends as we met them nearly every month. Some of them came from as far away as Cambridge and said they wouldn't miss the Felbrigg concerts for anything.

Chris's contention was that the music should be mostly familiar, with perhaps a few innovative pieces. Our audience wished to be entertained rather than educated, though they wouldn't be averse to meeting something new now and again.

With this in mind, he usually liaised closely with an artist over the content and, as the months passed, his vision was proved right: the concerts always sold out well in advance. Some people booked the entire season as soon as dates were announced.

The Morning Room makes an intimate concert hall. Because it can take, at most, seventy seats, there is no room for a large ensemble or a choir, so the choice of performer is important. There was no shortage of names on our list, and new ones were constantly sending details of their repertoires.

A favourite with both us and our audience was the young pianist Mark Bebbington. He delights every time he plays. One evening, knowing that a cancellation was coming up later in the season, Chris asked Mark if he could possibly fill in on that date with a different programme. Mark agreed at once, and when Chris announced the fact to that night's audience, nearly every one of them booked tickets for the next Mark Bebbington night.

We usually played host to the artists in our flat, providing them with a room to relax and change, and with refreshments. One Russian lady pianist was unhappy with the chill that pervaded Felbrigg in April; she was obliged to sit with her hands over a heater while she waited to begin, for fear her fingers wouldn't work properly.

A younger pianist arrived early with a problem: she had injured her back and needed to lie down for at least an hour before she could play. And ... she held out a bag of frozen peas ... could I possibly put those in the deep freeze? They would make a good ice pack. She wouldn't hear of our trying to cancel the concert – certainly not! If we would just stand by with those peas, and perhaps if we could delay the start of the concert by about ten minutes, to let her get properly rested ...

When the audience had gathered, Chris went in to do his usual welcoming speech and to tell them of the pianist's problem. Would they mind waiting ten minutes before the concert started?

No, not at all. They were concerned for the young lady, and quite happy sitting there.

'Perhaps I could tell you a few Felbrigg stories ...' said Chris.

His fund of tales was almost endless. Many times he kept groups either enthralled or in stitches. This evening was no exception. But in the middle of one particular tale he saw me signalling that the pianist was ready, so he stopped short and introduced her. Later, over a candlelit supper in the restaurant, someone complained that Chris hadn't finished his story, so he regaled them with it over the food and wine.

One concert memory that always makes us laugh is of the evening when Chris had booked a soprano, a lovely lady with a beautiful voice which would have sounded magnificent in the Albert Hall. Unfortunately, in our Morning Room it was a touch LOUD. At the interval, a young couple approached Chris and said rather sadly that they were afraid they would have to leave.

'Is something wrong?' Chris asked.

'Well, no, not really . . .' The lady was flushed as she indicated her pregnant bulge. 'It's just that I'm afraid she's disturbed the baby. He's kicking me to death. I'm not sure whether it's in enjoyment or protest. We really would love to hear the rest of the concert, but . . .'

Chris organized them some chairs out in the lobby, where they could see the singer but the baby would not be quite so disturbed by her volume, which she toned down for the second half.

A couple of months later, the same young pair visited the Hall on an open day when I happened to be selling tickets. They had come to show us their baby – a dear little boy with a shock of dark hair. I sent for Chris to come and see him; he adores babies.

'Do you think he'll be a music-lover?' we asked the proud parents, and they laughed. 'We'll be interested to find out!'

Still creeping . . .

No one suspected the unwelcome new member who had joined the Felbrigg team . . . the hidden menace of the dry rot, reaching out to fasten its thready fingers ever further in old woodwork and brick . . .

5

Celebrations

As summer ends and autumn starts to gild the edges of the trees, the pace of Felbrigg life slows a little and house staff have time to take a breath and perhaps contemplate snatching a few days away, a luxury not possible during the height of the season. One October we enjoyed a break in Nottingham, where Andrew had been at the university for several years doing a Ph.D. in chemistry. His efforts now culminated in the awarding of his doctorate; naturally we were very proud to see him in his robes. The event gave us a chance for a family get-together because, by coincidence, Kevin and his wife were then also living in Nottingham, both on the nursing staff at the City Hospital.

After that personal interlude, Felbrigg events again demanded our full attention, beginning when we hosted a small celebration to launch Sara Paston-Williams's *National Trust Book of Fish Cookery*. Sara herself was on hand to sign copies of her book and Joan produced samples of some of the mouth-watering recipes, of which local variations included Stookey Blues (cockles from Stiffkey) in Garlic; Blakeney Dabs with Samphire (a type of seaweed, delicious); Boiled Herring; Brancaster Staithe Oysters and, of course, the famous Cromer Crab. Many of that day's visitors milled about the buffet table, chatting with Sara before hieing off to the shop to buy (we hoped) the book.

Another year, as the season waned through October we had the pleasure of opening the new sixty-seat Park Restaurant, whose building had gone on all through the summer. It was not entirely complete. Behind it lay two or three private gardens which our tenants, would, reluctantly, have to give up; the area was needed as a service road for the restaurant, plus a courtyard with staff parking, garages for residents and sheds for the gardeners' equipment. Several months must pass before the work was finished but the restaurant itself was ready to open, adding waitress service to our list of assets.

In its first few weeks, apart from normal opening, the Park Restaurant was kept busy as the venue for a series of launching events, the first a brief drinks party for all staff and volunteers, to let everyone have a look at the handsome restaurant and the spacious, gleaming kitchens with stainless steel equipment and all the latest fittings. Then came the official opening, overseen by the regional director, with invited guests and the press there to publicize the new venture with a big central spread in the local paper. That same evening we threw a farewell party for the tenant of Home Farm, who was retiring to Madeira; and at the end of the week we held a cocktail party when many friends of Felbrigg came along to help us christen the restaurant. All this on top of our usual opening routine. Joan and her staff were especially busy.

Between them, Joan and Chris had come up with a couple of extra ideas to let people know about the Park Restaurant – a Celebration Lunch and a Hallowe'en Supper. For the latter, fancy dress was optional. Joan and her staff wore witches' hats, decked the restaurant in suitably spooky fashion and provided a spicy menu. Once again, Chris and I enjoyed ourselves dressing up, I as a witch with purple hair and green teeth, he as Count Dracula with all the trimmings. We thought it would add extra hilarity to the evening, which it did. Unfortunately this event, which we had hoped would become an annual feast, was stopped after its second year by some good folk who complained that we were toying with dark forces.

The NT and the NC

A group of teachers from schools in the area had asked if they might hold one of their meetings at Felbrigg and if Chris would address them on the facilities the National Trust could offer in response to the needs of the National Curriculum. Having been booked for this talk some months ahead of the date, Chris had put much thought and effort into it, even managing to get hold of a copy of the curriculum, which had proved more difficult than he had anticipated. He had had to order it from a bookshop in Norwich and wait weeks for its delivery.

When the day came he was apprehensive about having to address a roomful of professional lecturers, but he was well prepared with facts and full of ideas for ways in which Trust properties might be used to help children learn about history, from school trips to drama and role-playing, the possibilities of handling artefacts, in-depth study of special local issues . . . the list went on.

His audience sat in what he feared was a silence born of boredom, but afterwards the teachers told him they had been stunned to find that he knew more about the new curriculum than they did; they had had no idea that the Trust would be so co-operative; he had really fired their enthusiasm and started them thinking. They all wanted to enrol their schools in the Trust's School Membership system to ensure that they would receive all relevant details provided by the Educational Adviser.

Over tea, and during the tour of the house that followed, Chris was able to enlarge on some of his ideas and demonstrate how they might be carried out in practice. He had taken many school parties round and had kept their attention by telling the facts in an amusing and yet informative way, to stimulate young imaginations. It was a task he always enjoyed. Being upfront in the effort to help schools was, he believed, part of his task as administrator, as was the trouble he had taken in preparing for the teachers' meeting. You wouldn't find that listed on his job description but, for Chris, doing whatever is required of him to the best of his ability has always been a basic philosophy of life.

Hurricane humming

The night of 16 October 1987 – remember it? It was the night of the hurricane that devastated the south of England. But what no one south of Watford seemed to realize was that the storm swept on further north, diagonally across East Anglia, wreaking more havoc as it went. At about 6 a.m. on Friday, 17 October, wild winds woke us, battering around the Hall, a storm of sound and fury and driving rain. We felt the house shake and heard noises as of slates falling, but in the darkness we could see little.

My mother was staying with us at the time, still shocked, as we all were, by the sudden death of my father only six weeks before. She was in the usually cosy little Red Room guest suite. When I went to see how she was faring with the storm raging outside, I found poor Mum wide awake and glad to see me: the storm was battering directly against her shuttered window, and when I switched on the light we saw water pouring in across her windowboard. We staunched the flow with towels and, deciding to give the storm best, we all got up and made the good old English cure-all – some tea – to keep us going until dawn came.

Kevin was with us, too, sleeping in the Brown Room, also forced awake by the howling and blustering outside. He and Chris went to check the house as best they could in the dark. More water was seeping into the attics, being driven in around the old leads, and as the sky lightened, with the wind unabated, we saw broken slates in the courtyard outside. The trees in the park were sadly battered, some with branches torn off. Staring out at the devastation, we saw a bedraggled cock pheasant huddled against the front fence, held there by the force of the wind. It staggered off, carried by the gale, unable to fly.

Then at 7.30 a.m. the electricity went off, leaving us without power, though the cut lasted only until eleven, so we were lucky – in some places in remoter Norfolk, the power cut lasted a week.

Around eight o'clock, when the wind subsided a little, Chris went out to see what damage had been done. Apart from a few slates hurled from the roof, the house was in remarkably good shape. But he was concerned about the donkeys in the paddock. Tom, the woodsman, had gone to check on them, too, and finding them unharmed he and Chris stood for a while talking about the storm. Half an hour later, when Chris went back that way, he was horrified to see a tree lying just where he and Tom had been standing.

The worst of the hurricane was past by nine o'clock, the storm blowing itself out over the North Sea. In its wake, Chris and the outside staff assessed the damage, and the danger that remained: even though the strongest gales and rain had passed over, the wind was still powerful enough to bring down trees whose roots had been loosened in the night's furore.

It seemed fortuitous that the storm had happened on a Friday – a closed day, so not too many visitors would be trying to come. The main drive was totally blocked, as was the Lion's Mouth when Chris drove out to check them. Most of the other estate roads were clear, but soon after he passed along the Metton Road an entire copse went down and closed it. Days later we went by the spot and saw forlorn pheasants wandering bemusedly as if still unable to understand what had become of their nesting places in that wood, which was now just a mess of undergrowth and fallen trunks, edged by sawn-off chunks where the road blockage had been cleared.

Our most important immediate task was to get the public roads open; our main drive would have to wait until last. Our own men, and some from outside firms, set to at once to clear the Lion's Mouth. Chris was there when a family came sightseeing: he warned them away, telling them of a loose electric cable that was sparking and whipping in the wind nearby, and of the danger in the woods with the gale still strong and many trees teetering. The family ignored him – they wanted to see for themselves.

As soon as the Lion's Mouth had been cleared, traffic could at least reach the Hall by the back route. However, Chris put a notice by the rear lodge warning vehicles that there was as yet no through road: the front drive was still blocked and looked likely to be so for some time.

Twenty-five mature oaks had gone down like skittles, falling right across the entrance drive. *Twenty-five* of them, leaving great gaps in what had once been a beautiful archway of trees stretching from the main gate to the corner where a glorious copper beech grows. Kevin posed for photos among the felled giants and we still have the pictures. The trees are lying so closely packed that you can't even see there's a roadway.

Another sightseer came through, this time in a car. Arriving at the blockage, he proceeded to berate Chris in four-letter terms, telling him we should have had contingency plans, and why weren't there notices? When Chris pointed out that there *was* a notice at the far gate, which he must have seen as he passed, the man became even more abusive and made the ultimate threat: 'I shall write to head office and complain! You ought to be prepared for these emergencies! It's not good enough!' Shout as he would, it didn't move the trees; he was obliged to back off and go out the way he had come.

By the following morning it was clear that we might be wise not to try to open the house that day, either. Some of our volunteers who were due to be on duty could not get through because of trees still lying across their route. One lady had an oak down right across the front of her garage; she couldn't even open the doors to get at her car. But Joan had said she could manage to come in to open an abbreviated version of the tearoom, if I would help her, so Chris decided to tell other staff to stay away; he put up notices informing visitors that only the tearoom was open, and that the front drive was still blocked.

Few people came to visit that day. Joan left early and I manned the tearoom until closing time, with willing help from my mother. (*Everybody* gets roped in at Felbrigg!) But on the driveways the men kept on working, using chainsaws to hack the trees into movable pieces, which were then hauled away and stacked. The main drive was cleared by five o'clock and by Sunday it was business as usual, with only some areas of the woods posted as 'no go' because of half-uprooted trees that might topple.

But oh! the decimation of all the nearby woods and copses. Everyone who knew and loved Felbrigg's trees was appalled by the damage. But Nature soon managed to cover up the scars. To see it today, you would never believe what havoc was done by that storm.

At Blickling, the ornamental gardens had been struck by the gale and the results were painfully visible to everyone. Our own gardens, fortunately, remained unharmed but for the loss of a tree or two; most of the destruction at Felbrigg was deep in the woods, unseen by most casual visitors but equally devastating and equally expensive to put right. Nor were we alone. A special supplement in the local paper told of the frightful damage wrought across Norfolk to houses, barns, churches, gardens and farm crops. Yet when we spoke to Andrew, and my sister, on the phone, they were both amazed to hear that we had been in the hurricane's path – the national news had only reported what happened in Kent, and London.

In the wake of the hurricane, our friends who lived in the spacious Retreat, off the grass courtyard, organized a coffee morning and bring-and-buy/bric-à-brac sale to raise money to buy new trees. For days beforehand people were bringing their offerings and many kind helpers lent a hand to get them all laid out in various rooms of Gill and Henry's abode. They had put up posters asking for support from those who loved the woods, especially those who walked their dogs there regularly. The response was tremendous. Over two hundred people came. In less than three hours they raised £1000 – an astonishing sum for a coffee morning.

'Thank goodness everyone didn't turn up at once!' Henry said, ruefully regarding the chaos that was his home. It had been hectic for him and Gill. At times they had feared they might run out of space – or, worse still, coffee – but somehow they had managed. The result only showed how much people mourned the damage to the woods.

Two years after the hurricane, the local branch of the National Trust Volunteers celebrated its tenth birthday by clearing and replanting some of the Felbrigg trees. They will take a century to grow as tall as the ones that fell before the force of the great gale of '87.

After the wind, the rain

One of the worries in a great old house like Felbrigg is that damp may seep in, often in some unsuspected area. If it is not detected, it can cause untold, and expensive, damage, which is why Chris was often to be seen outside, during rainstorms, clad in a waterproof and carrying binoculars which he would train on the upper areas of the Hall. No, not a mad birdwatcher checking for house martins' nests, but an administrator looking for leaks in the gutters and downpipes. You can only spot them when it's really pouring with rain.

The problem is that the old downpipes are narrow, easily blocked with leaves or perhaps a dead bird. Sometimes when rain is deluging down you can't tell whether a pipe is blocked or whether it's spouting over because of the force of water. If in doubt, you must get someone to climb a ladder and find out.

Another way of checking for leaks is to get into the voids under the eaves. One at Felbrigg can be entered by a small trapdoor off the attic stairs, beyond which lies an aperture where a man can, with difficulty, wriggle along, carrying a torch to check for signs of wet coming in. Mind you, it's not for the squeamish. When Chris was in there he found his nose and mouth constantly covered with a fine netting of old cobwebs, though fortunately it wasn't until he emerged into the light that he saw the full extent of the filth he had been collecting – ancient spider's webs, dried dead flies, dust ... he was caked in them. He had a bath straight away, but felt unclean for days.

Something for everyone

People who visit old country houses often have a special interest in one particular aspect of the building or its contents. For some it may be the furniture, for others the paintings, or the porcelain, or perhaps the architecture. One retired foundryman was fascinated by the ironwork of the fireplaces at Felbrigg. For me, if I had to choose, what attracts me most are the human stories of the people who once inhabited the house – and, indeed, the living people who still come and go there. I am desperately sad for poor little 'Gla', who grew up to become 'Mad' Windham, and I should have loved to meet the five lively Ketton girls – Rachel Anna, Margaret, Ellen, Marion and Gertrude, who had the attics as their bedrooms in the 1860s. The last squire, Robert Wyndham Ketton-Cremer, was Rachel Anna's grandson and I wish I could have met him; he could have told me much I long to know.

Another family character of diverting interest never came to Felbrigg, as far as I know, though her story is part of the family history. In the sixteenth century, Florence Wadham married into the Wyndham (with a 'y') clan, in Somerset. A year after the wedding, she was buried with great ceremony in the family vault in St Decuman's Church at Watchet, much mourned by her young husband, John.

In the small hours of that same night, the local sexton stole down to the vault and opened her coffin, wanting to get at the valuable rings she was still wearing. Perhaps the rings were tight. The grave-robber decided to hack off her finger. But when the knife bit it drew blood, and Florence awoke! The terrified sexton fled, leaving behind his lantern, with which Florence lit her unsteady way back across the fields to her home and her astounded family. She survived to produce a son, from whom most of the surviving Wyndhams descend. I wonder what traumas she must have suffered, to wake up and find herself lying in a coffin in the family vault. Lucky she wasn't buried in the ground!

Whether this tale is apocryphal or not (a very similar story is told in France, concerning a French noblewoman), it appeals to my story-teller's instincts, as do many of the human tales linked with Felbrigg.

Whatever your passion – from embroidery to gardening, social history to architecture, cookery to fine art – you're bound to find something of interest in a stately home.

However, a lady who didn't have time to find *anything* of interest was once seen hastening through the bedrooms at 1.32 p.m. Since we had not opened the main door until half past one, she must have sped through the ground floor and up the stairs in two minutes flat. It was Sallie who, concerned, stepped out and asked if something was wrong.

'Yes, there certainly is,' cried the lady in distress. 'Just look at the colour of your guide book. And your dining room's the same. Horrible. Horrible!' And she hurried on, to be seen no more.

The guide book's cover is a pleasantly dusty purple; the dining room décor is faded lilac. I wish I had had a chance to ask the lady what had disturbed her so.

Stillingfleet

Among the many colourful characters who have been connected with Felbrigg over the centuries is one Benjamin Stillingfleet (1702–71). He was a botanist, chiefly remembered as being the first to name such now-familiar plants as cocksfoot, quaking grass and sheep's fescue. His portrait may be seen hanging on the upper landing of the staircase hall at Felbrigg, although, alas, he is wearing white stockings and not the blue which, in his later life, distinguished members of the original 'Blue Stocking' group which met at Mrs Elizabeth Montague's soirées in Bath.

Fate seems to have been against the young Stillingfleet: he was born without fortune, his father having been 'cut off without a penny' by *his* father, the stern theologian Bishop Stillingfleet of Worcester. (One wonders what heinous sin Benjamin's father could have committed to be disinherited by the good Christian bishop.) However, after studying at Cambridge, where ill-luck or prejudice denied him the fellowship for which he had hoped, Benjamin was employed by his relative, Squire Ash Windham, of Felbrigg Hall, as a tutor to Windham's somewhat wayward son, William.

Alas for Stillingfleet, he was not destined for personal happiness. He fell in love with a local Norfolk beauty, Miss Anne Barnes of Northrepps, to whom he wrote daily. He was so enamoured that he often walked three miles across the dark fields at night simply for the delight of gazing at her candlelit window. His admiration was evidently returned, for Anne agreed to an engagement. Stillingfleet recorded his feelings in a poem, which is scratched on a window-pane in the Bird Corridor at Felbrigg. (Incidentally, this poem is not the only inscription to have been scratched on a Felbrigg pane: the window in the administrator's bathroom reveals a pithier message, of Anglo-Saxon brevity. The provenance of this less erudite message is, alas, lost to history.)

Stillingfleet's sad little poem (if you catch it in the right light and can decipher the writing) reads:

> Could Lammy look within my breast
> She'd find her image there exprest
> In characters as deep as here
> The letters of her name appear
> And like them ever will remain
> Till time shall break my heart in twain.

The last line was prophetic. When it became obvious that Stillingfleet had little ambition and would never rise higher than being a tutor, Anne ended the engagement.

To soothe Stillingfleet's broken heart, in 1738 his employer sent him on a protracted Grand Tour with his pupil and distant cousin, William Windham, then twenty-one.

It was the custom for the sons of the wealthy to complete their education by travelling to foreign parts. Having sampled the delights of Paris for weeks, or even months, the Grand Tourists would journey to Italy to gorge themselves on the cultural treasures of Rome and Florence, or Vienna, or the German courts. Many stayed in Switzerland, and some travelled thence down the Rhine for a sojourn in the Low Countries before finally returning home. But not many of them spent as long over it as Windham and his tutor, who stayed abroad for four years.

It was on this Grand Tour that William Windham II acquired most of the paintings which now hang in the Cabinet at Felbrigg. In due time, after he inherited the estate, he had the Cabinet remodelled specifically to set off his collection. He even had a favourite picture copied and enlarged to go above the fireplace – much as we might do with a holiday snap today.

As for Benjamin Stillingfleet, he spent the remainder of his life partly in Bath and partly on the estates of various friends around the country, where he continued to indulge his passion for botany and became known for his erudition on the subject. He never did marry, but lavished affection on the children of his widowed sisters.

A modern 'Grand Tour'

Thames Television planned to produce a series of seven half-hour programmes following a fictional Grand Tourist on his journeyings and, perhaps because of Windham II's well-known adventures, they had arranged to do several days' filming at Felbrigg in November. This was to include sequences at the front of the house as the unnamed 'traveller' came and went, with more scenes in the Cabinet. But the star of the rooms was to be the Library again, from which every episode was introduced by the historian, and co-writer of the scripts, Christopher Hibbert.

The Thames TV 'traveller' was the actor Nicholas Gecks, who looked rather fine in his eighteenth-century costume, with a frilly white shirt and white silk stockings to go with his breeches. I got to know that shirt and those stockings fairly well since, discovering problems with doing laundry in the place they were staying, the props lady enlisted my help in washing and drying them each night. She rewarded me with a gift of toiletries before she left, though it was a chore I was pleased to do.

I went to watch some of the filming in the Library, where Christopher Hibbert was having difficulty getting his tongue round the convoluted introductory sentence someone had written on an 'idiot board'. I longed to suggest a rewording that might have helped, but held my peace: suggestions from outsiders were not welcome, as Chris had discovered when, overhearing a discussion between writer and director about the setting up of the Library shot, he had suggested that they might employ the two large globes which reside in the Library – a celestial globe showing a map of the sky and a terrestrial globe of the earth; perhaps if they turned the latter so it showed Europe . . . ? The director gave him such a look – interfering amateur! However, next day Chris saw the two globes placed as he had suggested, and each opening shot was of the terrestrial map, with Europe uppermost, opening out to reveal the traveller's hand writing in his journal, which he closed to reveal the title 'The Grand Tour'.

Fame at last!

Although the Hall was closed for the winter when this filming took place, the restaurant and shop remained open, so when film extras were needed, we in the house and Joan and her ladies were recruited to take the part of summer visitors, walking into the Cabinet, looking about as people will ... Our big moment came on screen at the very end of the series when, having completed his Grand Tour and returned home again, the traveller stood in the Cabinet admiring his collection of art treasures culled from various stops on his journey. Nick's figure faded out, revealing the same Cabinet, but with today's visitors coming and going.

Fame at last! For all of two seconds.

'Beyond the Baize Door ...'

Once he became administrator, Chris was able to bring to fruition an idea which had long been forming in his mind: special guided tours of Felbrigg's attics and cellars. These areas are not normally open to the public; they present their own safety hazards and security problems, which make regular opening impossible. But they are so interesting that he wanted to show them to a few more people, to widen understanding and appreciation of the house and the way in which it was used down the centuries. The attics in particular are full of fascinating memorabilia which, while not of great intrinsic value, are of endless interest to anyone the least drawn to history and the minutiae of other people's lives – those of us who are nosy, in fact, and like rummaging in other people's odds and ends.

When we first arrived, the attics had not been sorted out for years. There had been no time. Since the Trust took over in 1969–70, efforts had been concentrated on the gradual opening up of the main rooms and the modernization of facilities, and, anyway, no manpower had been available to do the extra work required. Chris was the first houseman employed at Felbrigg; until then the place had been run by a married couple – the man looking after the house and administration while his wife managed the small shop and tearoom and also sold tickets. It was a very low-key operation compared with what it has developed into today but, even so, it left the custodians no time to worry about the attics.

When Chris had a chance to examine those rooms under the eaves, he found them crammed to bursting with all manner of furniture and bric-à-brac, some left as the family had stored it long ago, more pushed in while Trust personnel were preparing the state rooms for public viewing. Some of the attics could hardly be accessed at all: the stuff inside was packed so untidily you could hardly squeeze round the door.

As I told in *Cobwebs and Cream Teas*, in spare moments at winter weekends and after duty in the evenings, Chris had slowly been organizing the attics so their contents were in more comprehensible order. For instance, one room now held all the spare chests, another had mainly beds, another area stored chairs and yet another was a repository for linen. This last was mainly stored in a giant wardrobe which had been in bits and pieces all over the place. Chris had gradually gathered it together and reconstructed it, a wonderful mahogany monster with two huge mirrors concealing an abundance of cupboards and drawers. Dolly, one of our cleaners, had fallen in love with the wardrobe and asked to be allowed to polish it back to shining glory, which she did. This magnificent piece of furniture is kept now under dust sheets, and, yes, it is a shame it can't be displayed, but we have one just like it in one of the bedrooms and there's no room for another. The same can be said for many of the interesting items in the attics: it would be marvellous to have them on permanent display, but at present there is nowhere to put them. Maybe one day there might be a museum room, perhaps in the lock-up area – another of Chris's ideas for the future.

The chairman of our local National Trust Volunteers had said that he and his friends would love a chance to see the attics. 'If ever I get to be administrator . . .' Chris had promised. Hardly had he taken over than Roger was on the 'phone: 'You remember you said you'd give us a look round your attics and cellars . . .' So they came, and they, too, were amazed by the wonders that had formerly lurked unseen.

To test the idea further, Chris sent out a general invitation to staff and volunteers to come and visit us one summer evening and have a guided tour. Most of them had never seen beyond the public rooms and were thrilled by the opportunity to learn more about the house. This included a grand tour of our flat, which we threw open for viewing, also serving drinks and nibbles in our big sitting room.

That event was a huge success, but then we had half expected it – all our guinea pigs so far had been Felbrigg enthusiasts. Less predictable was whether other people would feel the same about the projected special tours. It would be a risk, but worth trying, if only once.

During one of his frequent talks to local groups, Chris had mentioned his idea and later the chairman had asked whether he and his association might book an 'attics and cellars evening', with a supper to follow. Chris naturally agreed: it meant extra revenue plus the chance to test out the special tour with people who were not well acquainted with the house. When that, too, proved a highly satisfying evening, he knew he was ready to launch what he eventually titled 'Beyond the Baize Door . . .'

The tours took place during two weeks in November, after the fully occupied routine of normal opening days and before the equally crammed schedule of winter cleaning. During that fortnight the cleaners are busy removing and storing away all the smaller items, then covering the furniture with dust covers. It usually takes a full two weeks to accomplish this operation before they start the annual cleaning, which begins, as a rule, in the attics.

Chris had spent hours going over the logistics of having four separate parties around the house and managing to keep them moving smoothly, with no bottle-necks and mix-ups. We sent out explanatory leaflets with booking forms, so that people knew what they were in for: we couldn't take children under twelve; others must be fairly fit to climb all the stairs – there are five flights to the attics; they should wear sensible shoes to cope with uneven terrain, and they should bring a torch, there being no lights in some areas. They should also be prepared for dust and cobwebs, and aware of the need to listen to and obey the guides at all times as some places could be dangerous if someone was careless.

Chris and I worked on the instruction leaflet until we felt we had covered everything that might be of concern. Even so, we had a phone call from one lady who was 'most keen to come', but, as she wasn't too good on her legs, 'could you please confirm that the attics are all on the ground floor?'

Each group had two guides, one in front to lead and do most of the talking, one bringing up the rear to shepherd stragglers and answer any other queries. The guides were well rehearsed and equipped with a timetable which they knew must be strictly followed. We met twice for a briefing run-through under instruction from Chris, who was literally the only person in the world then equipped to organize and lead these tours.

I, naturally, was one of the guides – wouldn't have missed it for worlds. Much as I groaned at times about the intrusion into our privacy and the interruption to my writing, I couldn't keep from getting involved in whatever was going on. And I loved every minute of those special tour days. The visitors were so excited by what they were seeing, so absorbed and enthused, that it was a delight to be part of it. We were only sorry we couldn't do more. We could have sold the tickets ten times over.

Because these tours were the first of their kind, they attracted tremendous publicity. Both of our local papers printed big picture features and Anglia Television came and gave the event enthusiastic coverage. Unfortunately, by the time the first features came out that year's two tours had ended, but people were calling from all over the country wanting to buy tickets. We had to tell them to send in their names for next year's waiting list.

On 'Baize Door' days, visitors would start arriving an hour or more before we opened the Hall's main door. They had been advised that we started *promptly* at ten, with no leeway for latecomers as our schedule was so tight: once we had started no one would be available to answer the door to the tardy. So they came in good time, not to miss anything. If it was fine, Chris would go out into the front courtyard and give them a brief orientating chat about the Hall and the areas we were going to see. Then we all gathered in the Morning Room, where he told them which group they were with, introduced the guides and explained the special instructions necessary for everyone's safety. Great care had to be taken on uneven cellar stairs, under sloping ceilings and low doorways, and in places where they must keep to the designated route, especially in the attics where a false step could send them plunging down a void.

'Of course, if you *really* feel the need to get to the cellars quickly,' he would say, 'that's up to you. It's only sixty feet or so.'

Next, is everyone sensibly shod? Have all brought torches, as per ticket instructions? Has everyone been to the relieving station? – no loos in the attics. Good. He wants them to be safe and comfortable. They do know that there are a lot of stairs, don't they?

One lady, who admitted to having a bad heart, frightened us by insisting she could do the whole tour. She did, too, but not without a lot of stops for breath and much anxiety on our part. 'I was *determined* to see your attics,' she said. 'Might never have another chance.'

Let me take you in imagination on one of these special tours, with Chris in the lead and me bringing up the rear. We are doing the main house tour first, following the usual route, but seeing how the state rooms are now going under wraps, dust covers on the furniture and acid-free paper wrapping the bronzes. Chris explains how each cleaning process has special techniques, how the carpets and fabrics are vacuumed very gently through a fine mesh and the chandelier taken apart drop by crystal drop, washed, dried and rehung. Our cleaners are conservators, too, skilled in the preferred methods laid down by the Trust over years of experience.

In a friendly, relaxed atmosphere people ask questions as we go along the west wing to the Cabinet, where Chris tells about the Grand Tour, and the time we had John Bligh (of *Antiques Roadshow* fame) here for a day's filming with Lady Victoria Leatham from Burleigh House. Then he turns his torch to the ceiling to show exactly where the little animals are hidden among the plaster ornamentation. This brings exclamations of surprise and delight, and 'Where? I can't see them', from the short-sighted.

On we must press, into the corridor and back towards the staircase hall, Chris chatting all the way.

Up in the Library the three cleaners (yes, just *three* ladies manage to keep this entire house pristine) are dusting and checking the books, taking them down, with care, a few at a time. Dolly, Margaret and Susan thoroughly enjoy this chance to meet visitors face to face: usually their work is carried out while the house is quiet, long before visitors come in, so this is their opportunity to share the joy of answering questions and exercising their expertise.

We could spend ages talking about the books, but, keeping a close eye on the clock, we head along the landing and down the back stairs, only a minute or two behind time. On the ground floor we make again for the front of the house, passing another animated group in the Bird Corridor.

The route to the older cellars lies under the administrator's flat, down narrow, rickety wooden steps and a couple of twisting stone stairs to a maze of empty, echoing rooms and passages smelling of age, damp and dust. It is gloomy down there, lit only by an inspection lamp, which we have fixed up on the wall, and by the beams of our torches. See this huge, solid door, cut down to fit the opening, with a metal grille in it? We speculate whether the room beyond, down three steep steps, might once have been a strong room. It is now fitted with wooden racks meant to hold barrels, and it has a drain-hole in its floor, for the convenience of whoever used to sluice the floor down. Look up through another grille and you can see into the Bird Corridor above.

Further on – watch that electric cable on the floor! – another empty, echoing sideroom has a barrel ceiling, with a lot of graffiti on it, old and not so old. Workmen, and others who get the opportunity, love to scribble their names in such places. You can just see the curve in the ceiling where once the stairs came down from the buttery (now the Morning Room).

As we go deeper towards the front of the house, take care over the trailing cable from the light which Chris is now holding. He leads the way through a narrow arched passage, past a place where toads crawl against a window, safe in their home under a grille in the front courtyard. Down a couple of uneven steps now, and into the very oldest cellar, which we believe may once have been the undercroft of the medieval manor. How old it is we aren't sure, perhaps fourteenth century or even earlier, but we do know it leads out under the front courtyard, and it's usually damp, with water dripping.

Torchlight penetrates the deeper recesses as people crane to see every crevice. Iron rings in the ceiling once held lanterns. You can see from the black dust that at some time coal was stored here. Light catches on beads of wetness that gather in the curved roof and plop coldly on to your head. Toads and lizards crawl on the floor, and in the walls you can see the bore holes someone has drilled, trying to discover what lies under the Great Hall. Solid rubble was all the holes revealed.

Right, back now to the steps. Mind the cable! Mind your heads! Careful on the wooden steps!

To reach the other cellars we go back through the Bird Corridor, pausing to look at Stillingfleet's poem etched on the glass. In a lobby by the foot of the back stairs we point out the iron ring in the ceiling, for hauling barrels up and down through the huge trapdoor some of you are standing on. This door here under the stairs leads to the wine cellars. More stone steps. Mind how you go!

The wine cellars are better lit, except for the last two rooms which still contain the 'bins', lined with sawdust that still bears the imprint of bottles, and hung with lead labels whose names evoke an era of rich living. Shine your torch and read out the names – Madeiras, brandies and ports; Morel's Champagne 1852, Barnes's East Indian Sherry 1829 . . .

The only remaining bottles, a few old stone flasks, lie on the floor in a corner, tightly sealed and still containing something liquid, as you can hear when you shake them. They are inscribed 'Herzogthum, Nassau'. We did wonder if they might hold rum from the West Indies, but when Chris opened one of the flasks, for the benefit of television cameras, he was disappointed to discover it was only seltzer water. Quite palatable and still slightly fizzy, but not very inspiring.

Still answering questions, we must start up to the Old Kitchen, where Joan will have our coffee waiting. Coffee break is always the time for great animation, discussing what we have seen so far and asking more questions.

Fifteen minutes later we're off again, this time up the back stairs, winding and twisting all the way to the attics. Arthritic knees crack, rheumatic joints ache, breath comes swift and hoarse – some of the visitors are almost as bad!

Up in the attics the corridors are narrow, the ceilings slope to one side, and it is poorly lit by the odd window here and there. First we will go into the most northerly room, where we keep the frames and springs of spare beds. This room has a tiny fireplace, its surround shaped like a large horse-shoe – someone once told us that this was because the grooms slept here, which can't be true because the children of the house occupied these attics and it is unlikely that the squire would have let his rough, unlettered male grooms anywhere near his darling daughters.

Only in town houses did the servants use the attics. In the country many of the servants lived out, with their families on the estate. At Felbrigg, the grooms had their quarters over the stables, while other menservants slept in rooms above the servants' hall, which is now the shop. The maids lived over the Old Kitchen, guarded by the housekeeper. The attics were reserved for the squire's children, and perhaps a governess or nurserymaid. No, the squire and his lady didn't often use the grand bedrooms in the west wing – those were kept for special guests. The squire's private quarters were more or less where our flat is now.

Each room in the attics has its own delights. Where that lovely mahogany wardrobe has pride of place, full of linen, there is also an old, much-loved and rather threadbare lion on wheels. 'He'll still talk to us,' says Chris as he pulls the string to make the lion give his endearing growl.

'Goodness,' one chap comments. 'You could hold a wonderful car boot sale with this lot, couldn't you?'

'It would have to be a Rolls-Royce boot sale!' someone else laughs.

Next is the room reserved for pictures, where Chris rediscovered a couple of valuable watercolours, and then the chair area – see that ancient basketwork wheelchair? – and then a large room at the front, the only other one with a fireplace, possibly once a schoolroom? It now contains chests of drawers where are stored all manner of secrets, including a collection of vicious-looking antique swords.

Here, the dormer window opens out on to the leads behind the parapet. Chris invites those who wish to follow him through the narrow opening to take a better look at the view from that height. Most of the visitors want to go, even though it is less than elegant for some ladies, scrambling up the steps, sticking one leg out to the short ladder beyond, squeezing through the window opening and then being handed down to the leads below. But oh! the view, and the tales Chris has to tell . . .

On one rather dark and windy day, a lady had been in a bad mood ever since she arrived. All the way round she had been complaining to her companion about something or other. Now, refusing to go out on to the roof in the wind, as Chris launched into another anecdote she sighed irritably, 'More tall tales!'

'I promise you,' I said, 'everything Chris has told you is true. We don't need to invent stories. You just have to live here and it all happens around you.'

I'm not sure she believed me. However, even she was impressed by the final room where, by the light of one of our shadeless bedroom lamps, fixed to yet another long cable which snaked up from our flat, Chris showed the group the assortment of toys we keep here – ludo and draughts, a small boat, a whole boxful of games we've never had time to examine. Here, too, are copies of Victorian *Punch* magazines, a chest of small drawers where someone's collection of fossils and medallions is kept, an asseyor's scales neatly packed in a box, an old map of the estate . . . a bewilderment of objects so diverse that not even Chris has ever managed to look at them all in detail. He always puts on a great show at this point, like a magician producing wonders from a hat. And all of these things were left here by some former occupant of the Hall. *That*'s what provides the extra touch of magic, the fact that everything belongs here, and adds to our intimate knowledge of Felbrigg.

Over lunch, the disgruntled lady found herself sitting next to Chris, whom I had forewarned, and by the time she left she, too, was smiling.

As a result of the immense interest engendered that first year, we didn't need to publicize future events: tickets were mostly spoken for before they were printed. To sell the last few, all we had to do was put up a notice in a corridor. One year we had a frantic telephone call from a Reuters' correspondent in London who said he just *had* to come on a special tour, why hadn't he heard about them before, why didn't we publicize it nationally, and couldn't we *please* squeeze him in? Chris might have made an exception as the caller was so desperate, but the last tour of that session was the following day and the man couldn't get to Norfolk in time; so he was disappointed. We even had to put an embargo against people coming two years' running. Some of them would have come every year if they could, because they found one tour wasn't nearly enough to take it all in.

Over the years the attics and cellars tours developed from those tentative beginnings. In later years we did six tours, spread over two weeks with lunch included, and in the final year we went all out with a full day's entertainment comprising 'Baize Door' tours in the morning, with a four-course gourmet lunch followed by a short break to take the air before Chris gave one of his by-then famous talks where he showed some of the more precious and unusual objects in detail. All tickets were sold out almost as soon as the event was announced, months in advance.

Some Trust houses do put on what they call 'Putting the House to Bed' occasions when visitors can see the property going under wraps and hear details about the winter cleaning. But Chris's 'Beyond the Baize Door . . .' days were, as far as we know, unique. We were fortunate in that Felbrigg's attics and cellars *were* so interesting, were also reasonably accessible, and contained so much material worthy of display and discussion. Other properties have empty attics; some are too cramped to make such events viable. And, of course, you need an administrator who knows his house from top to bottom, who is willing to take on the extra work that the organization of such events requires, and who can rely on the support of staff and volunteers alike.

One lady, who said she had had a wonderful time and could have spent hours and hours in our attics, was concerned about all the extra work the tours must mean. She helpfully suggested that in future, instead of having the events on Monday, Wednesday and Friday of each week, over two weeks, we might consider holding them from Monday to Saturday and get them all over in one week, 'to save locking up the house in between'. When I told her we locked up as a matter of routine, every day come what might, she was aghast. 'You mean . . . you actually go round locking up everything, every night – *even during the season*?!'

In the last year of our 'Beyond the Baize Door . . .' tours we charged more than usual for the tickets. Chris was concerned that the cost might be too steep, but we sold all the tickets without effort and no one complained that they hadn't had their money's worth. On the contrary, as I saw them out at the end of the afternoon, everyone was thoroughly satisfied and complimentary over the wonderful treat we had supplied. Four different people told me they had been given the tickets as a birthday present, and all of them said it was the best birthday present they had ever had.

Of all the things Chris tried to do for Felbrigg, the attics and cellars tours provided some of our most happy and rewarding memories. Perhaps in the future someone else may have the pleasure of leading similar parties. I hope so. I should love to go on one again myself.

Delicate dusting

Although our stalwart cleaners handle every book in the Library every winter, when they dust the edges and the covers and flick through to check for signs of mites or beetle which could destroy the valuable tomes, it had been a very long time – centuries in some cases – since anyone had had time to examine every page closely. That chore required the attentions of a specialist team, who arrived one winter to spend eight weeks working in the

Library. There are over five thousand books on the shelves at Felbrigg. In two months, the conservators hoped to deal with about half of the collection.

Before Caroline and her three colleagues began, the entire room was draped, dust sheets placed over bookcases and across the carpet to catch the detritus as the deepest recesses of each page were brushed clean. One page at a time, it was slow, painstaking, time-consuming work, but necessary if the precious books were not to be irrevocably damaged. The conservators used soft paintbrushes, working under spotlights so they could see clearly and get at every last bit of whatever scholars might have dropped into the books over the years. They identified particles of breadcrumb, leaf, tobacco and candle wax, not to mention flakes of human skin and the usual crop of dust and fluff. They hoped that their efforts would also remove any eggs of death watch beetle which might have been laid there, too small for the eye to see. We had already had an example of the kind of damage the creatures could wreak when one hatched out and began to eat its way from the spine to the edge, growing as it went . . . Luckily our cleaners found the miscreant before it bored through and flew off to lay yet more microscopic eggs.

While they were doing their cleaning, the conservation team would also repair torn pages and glue bent covers, refold book plates in their original creases and mend spine labels. Specially tailored slipcases were being made, too, to help support the more fragile books and prevent pages from crinkling. The cases were individually made, fitting to within a millimetre.

Felbrigg houses a real scholar's library, of well-used and well-loved books, read and enjoyed by our squires, not simply bought by the yard and put up for show, as was the case in some houses. They were mostly bound in calf, some in reverse calf, so the cover is white. This binding, and the pages, are easily damaged by oil and sweat from fingers, which is why house staff are required to wear cotton gloves when handling them. Some of them are extremely valuable. And because the spines are so easily torn, there's a special way to remove them from the shelves – you don't just stick your finger on top and pull, as we all do in public libraries, you reach in, over and behind the book,

We had already had an example of the kind of damage the death watch beetle could wreak, when one hatched out and began to eat its way from the spine to the edge, growing as it went . . .

gently easing it forward until it sticks out far enough for you to take firm hold of it.

To protect the books on our shelves from accidental damage by curious hands, we keep wires stretched across them so that the books can't easily be removed. But not everyone understands our purpose.

A Norfolk matron, in the Library one day, looked round with great interest, then asked her daughter, 'What's them there wires for, then?'

'Sssh, Mother,' said daughter, slanting an embarrassed smile at the nearby room warden. 'I expect they're there to stop people from stealing the books.'

Mother looked askance at the rows of ancient leather tomes, some of them faded, some a little worn. 'Why,' said she in scornful disbelief, 'whoever'd wanta pinch *them* old things?'

The chancer

Although our fire alarms sounded all too frequently because of some minor fault – before they were updated, that is – we could never afford to ignore them. But on the few occasions the intruder sirens blared, they had us especially on the alert. So far, they, too, had signalled only some minor problem, quickly solved. But we couldn't afford to be complacent. Each time, we had to act as though the emergency was genuine.

And so, when the sirens wailed and the deafening bells began to clamour at around 1.30 a.m. on a bleak November night, Chris and I tumbled out of bed, grabbed our dressing gowns and went down to check which area was affected. The signal told us the problem was in the Great Hall. Having established that, Chris switched off the main alarms – they are so loud you can't think – leaving just a buzzer sounding at the panel.

Eddie and Katie, also both in dressing gowns, rushed to join us from their more-distant quarters, bleary-eyed and dishevelled, just as we were. We peered at each other in the light of a lone electric bulb in a dismal private corridor with dark red, peeling walls.

'We'll go and see what's happening,' Chris said to Eddie, his great bunch of keys ready in his hand as he added to me, 'You and Katie stay here. At the first sign of trouble, close and lock this door and ring the police, just to make sure they're on the way.'

So Katie and I waited by the inner door while our husbands made their way across the front lobby, past the ticket desk, and unlocked the door of the Great Hall. Opening it cautiously, Chris shone his torch across the huge room and, seeing glass scattered over the carpet by one of the far windows, he swiftly closed and locked the door again. It was no time for false heroics, as he said later. If he had gone charging in, someone might have been waiting there with a shotgun to force him to give them access to the rest of the house. As it was, they couldn't get further than the room they were in. He and Eddie returned to where we were waiting and told us what they had seen.

'We'll just wait for the police,' Chris said. 'They'll be here any minute.'

'I'll go and wait for them by the back door,' Eddie offered.

Katie went off to put on something warmer and in the ensuing silence we realized that our phone was ringing upstairs in the flat. Perhaps one of the courtyard tenants was phoning to see if all was well. The burglar alarms don't usually sound in the small hours, after all.

I hurried up to our kitchen to answer the call. 'Felbrigg Hall.'

'Oh, hello,' came a young woman's voice. 'This is the police here. Did you know your alarms had gone off?'

Did we know . . . ?!

The ringing of the back-door bell sent me hurrying downstairs again hoping the police had arrived, but instead the caller was our new young woodsman, Gary, who had been woken by the alarm, had dressed hurriedly and come over to see if he could help. His large and cheerful presence was a welcome addition to our little group.

Two police officers arrived about fifteen minutes later.

The burglar had fled, without taking anything. He had broken a pane of the leaded window, reached in and opened the latch, and climbed through, perhaps assuming that because those windows were unshuttered they were also unguarded. He had soon learned better. We could see the mark on a marble table, where a muddy shoe had slid as he leaned on a bronze depicting Mercury. The bronze had bent, perhaps as the burglar overbalanced in his panic when the alarms blared. He had evidently taken hasty leave of us.

The police found the print of a trainer shoe outside, and later discovered a stolen motorbike abandoned in the middle of the drive by the Sexton's Lodge where our head gardener lives. Perhaps, they surmised, the chap had skidded and come off the bike in his haste and decided to run rather than try to restart his vehicle. Ted was not much amused to be woken and asked if the motorbike belonged to him – he was not in the habit of leaving machines sprawled in the middle of the main drive, in the middle of the night.

In the morning, fingerprint officers came and dusted round everywhere the intruder might have touched. It seemed he had acquired his transport in Norwich and, 'joyriding', had found himself in Felbrigg Park where he decided to try his luck. 'A chancer,' the police decided.

Whoever he was, to date they haven't found him.

Following this incident, a letter from on high sternly informed us that we must *be vigilant* and that we must be sure that, at this time of year, all valuables were secured away out of harm. They had been: they always were. The letter bemused us. How much more vigilant could we be?

Trying to carry out these instructions, a few days after the burglary Chris happened to be out just after nightfall when a car came through, the driver cruising along while his dog had a run beside him. Flagging the vehicle down, Chris explained that a by-law prohibited entry between dusk and dawn.

The trespasser's reaction was immediate: 'Who do you think you are, you stupid old man? I've been driving through here for years, and I'm not stopping now.'

Such abuse is par for the course. But that *old man* really hurt!

6

The year's waning

The advent of dark December days may change the pace of life at National Trust houses, but only to alter, not diminish it. Indeed, in winter when renovation and conservation are the priorities there is often more hassle and confusion than during the season, when we are cushioned by the regular routine.

Workmen proliferate, maybe a painter applying gloss and emulsion both in the shop passageway and in our flat, and more builders are busy outside preparing the service road to the rear of the Park Restaurant. Meanwhile, our cars have to be parked outside the stableyard, waiting for their new garages, so if you come in laden with shopping it's quite a trek to get it home. And if you arrive after dark, best have a torch ready – I've never seen dark as dark as it can be at Felbrigg.

The Morning Room is now taken up by the girl who is doing the next stage of the inventory, numbering and photographing every last item before retiring to her place of work to put all the photographs on cards, with written descriptions – a huge task that takes two years. Later, Eddie will have the equally daunting task of checking that all the numbers tally and descriptions are correct, a chore that has to be fitted in on top of all his other duties. A houseman's work is never done!

Elsewhere the annual cleaning is well into its routine by this time. The ladies will finish ridding the attics of a year's worth of cobwebs, dust, dead flies and mouse droppings before moving to the base camp, scrubbing it all through before it is closed up, the water and power turned off until spring. After that, they will begin on the main rooms of the house.

As the cleaners and the houseman take their annual close look at every inch of the house, they never know what new problem they may suddenly discover. It could be, and usually is, beetle in the books, chips in the porcelain, tears in fabric or carpets, woodworm which will have to be expensively treated ... Nature, and our visitors, each play a part in wear and tear. We need the winter break to put it all right, as far as we can.

Dry rot

You will remember the fungus that had settled in the Chinese Bedroom, spreading its tiny tentacles through brick and wood. Eventually it became so over-confident that it started to show itself. Our ever-vigilant cleaners were the first to notice a light drift of brown, powdery crumbs of wood coming from a crack between the top of the dado board and the wall. They reported it to Eddie, who informed Chris, who in turn went to investigate and realized with horror what it might be – he had come across those signs before.

When tested under a microscope by experts, the brown powder proved to be just what Chris had feared: the spores of a dry rot fruiting body. The first signs were discovered in September, but it was December before the work could begin. This may seem a long time, but it took three months to organize because, as ever, the job was not as simple as it might appear. To begin with, before investigating the extent of the trouble, the experts had to get at the wall itself, which meant that, first, the wallpaper had to be removed. In a normal house, this would be easy – you would simply damp the paper and scrape it off, cursing the mess, no doubt. But at Felbrigg even the wallpaper is precious, that in the Chinese Bedroom being nearly two and a half centuries old.

The Chinese Bedroom was remodelled during the programme of architectural changes which took place around 1750, in the squiredom of William Windham II. At the same time the Samwell-designed staircase (built in the 1680s) was removed and the stairwell area was turned into the present Dining Room, with the Grey Dressing Room and the Yellow Bedroom above, much as we know them today.

At the north end of the west wing, Windham II's architect, James Paine, added a bay window to the Cabinet and to the small bedroom above (now the Chinese Bedroom). Then he bricked over the existing west-facing windows in those rooms. The windows are still visible from outside, so the symmetry of line along the wing is not spoiled, but from inside both rooms all you see on that side are blank walls: the one in the Cabinet allows display of the largest of Windham's pictures, collected on the Grand Tour we noted earlier, while in the Chinese Bedroom Paine hung 'India paper'. This came, in fact, from China, via the East India Company. The same paper is still there today. Before it could begin to deal with the dry rot, the Trust had to find and employ someone capable of removing that precious, 240-year-old Chinese wallpaper *in such a way that it could be rehung once the job was finished*. Such a person is not to be found in every copy of the *Yellow Pages*, and when you do find one you have to join the queue waiting to benefit from his or her expertise.

Unlike our modern papers, Chinese wallpaper is made from bamboo canes or mulberry trees. Their long, tubular fibres are cross-hatched and pressed together, giving the finished paper enormous strength. It is cut into large sections forty-eight inches wide, and then hand-painted.

The Felbrigg paper is a glory of ducks, silver pheasants and birds of paradise sitting and strutting among bamboo trees, peonies and lotuses aflutter with butterflies. When the last squire died, it was in a bad state because of damp coming through the ceiling and in 1974 the Trust had the wallpaper removed, restored, and repainted in a few places. This removal disclosed a scribbled note which read '18 pictures birds and flowers, Mr Payne[sic]'. The wallpaper was then rehung on a lining of cartridge paper, which was considered the correct thing in those days. But knowledge of paper had moved on by the second removal and our expert, Orde Solomons, found his task made more difficult by that well-intended lining.

He had developed a tool of his own for his special work, an

electronic vapour hose which gave out steam at low pressure but high temperature, up to 180 degrees centigrade, which liquidized the glue but didn't unduly wet the paper. This instrument was inserted between the paper and the wall, and sections were painstakingly eased away as the glue softened. The old Chinese paper withstood the work well. It was the new cartridge lining that disintegrated into a pulpy mess.

The sections of the original wallpaper were layered in acid-free tissue and stored by rolling them in plain white paper. When the job was completed, Orde Solomons took the pieces back to London with him and kept them until it was time to restore and reline them.

When the entire west wall had been stripped and the wallpaper carefully taken away, Bullens' men moved in to start the filthy job of taking off the old lath and plaster and exploring the extent of the dry rot. We hoped it wouldn't be too bad, but when the brickwork was exposed it was clear the infestation had gone deep, not only into the wall but into the floor. The men removed a big section of floorboards to get at the joists, and knocked a great hole in the inner wall, exposing the old window, still with its wooden shutters fastened – fascinating, but rather like watching a surgeon expose your beloved granny's innards and hoping he can put her back together again. Only when every last extent of the dry rot had been revealed could they begin treatment. It was a long job which went on, at intervals, well into the next season.

Eventually, as summer was beginning, Orde Solomons returned to Felbrigg and rehung the sections of Chinese wallpaper in what he laconically described as 'the usual way' with wheat-starch paste. But this time he used a fabric liner which can be easily removed if ever the paper needs to be taken down again.

He did the job superbly. If you visit Felbrigg, check whether *you* can 'see the joins'.

Light in dark days

Though the Hall itself closes to the public at the end of October, the shop and restaurant remain open until Christmas, and at the beginning of December staff deck their halls with boughs of holly, and baubles, and other merry seasonal fripperies. People arrive to have hot mince pies with their coffee, and to browse over Christmas shopping in comfort, with a chance to blow away the winter blues by taking a walk in the park, away from the chaos of city centres.

We played our own part in giving the Hall a welcoming Christmas appearance by setting up a tree in the bay of our sitting room. Tom the woodsman supplied us with a huge tree which we set up, not without problems, on a sturdy table in the bay: the window was so high that if we had stood the tree on the floor only its top would have been seen from outside. Even so, it was so enormous that our own trimmings would cover only half of it – the half that showed from outside, of course. We had to go out and buy a lot more baubles and tinsel, and another set of lights, to cover the green branches that showed on our side. We almost needed a scaffold to complete it.

From the park the tree looked spectacular as the sun began to set on those winter afternoons and coloured lights spangled out a welcome from our window, sparkling on glitter and silver balls. Many people remarked on the sight it made, visible from a long distance as cars approached down the drive. We kept it lit all evening, through December, and it became a tradition at Felbrigg while we were there.

Like minds

Opportunities for social meetings with colleagues from other properties are limited. However, since we had all met at the administrators' conference at Madingley Hall, we had kept in touch by phone whenever business demanded it; we had run into each other at meetings, or when I had accompanied Chris on one of his Health and Safety visits, and, just occasionally, Chris and I had gone to another property as visitors during the season, taking a busman's holiday. Over the years, the other administrators had become friends.

And so, when it came to be our turn to host the annual Heads of Houses meeting, we invited the men to bring their wives for a change, and to come over and spend the night before the meeting. We thought it would be good to have a social get-together and an opportunity to talk at length about our mutual concerns. The others must have agreed – they all accepted. They came from Wimpole Hall and Anglesey Abbey in Cambridge-shire; Lavenham Guildhall in Suffolk; Oxburgh Hall in west Norfolk and, of course, from neighbouring Blickling Hall. Some of them stayed overnight with us, the rest with the administrator at Blickling.

That evening I made a simple dinner and we sat long into the night in our sitting room, exchanging ideas, successes, gripes and grievances, as colleagues do. We all enjoyed discovering that we shared so many experiences. Next morning, while the men had their first official meeting in the Morning Room, we women went off shopping and had lunch at a coffee shop. We didn't suspect that, back at Felbrigg, a partial power-failure had occurred and, as it happened to affect the Morning Room area, the men had been getting colder and colder. Chris was the last to realize – he had become inured to the bitter air of what is reputed to be the coldest house in Norfolk!

By the time we returned, the afternoon meeting was well under way – in our flat, as I discovered when I walked in and found the East Anglia administrators and the regional director all seated at our dining table. Fortunately the electricity in our quarters was still on.

Having been told about the lack of heat in the Morning Room, I returned to my friends in the kitchen and we made the men some tea. All of us went in to serve it and I treasure the look of astonishment on the regional director's face when he realized that all the wives were there as well as the men. But he did say our getting together was a good idea, and he suggested we should do the same every year – perhaps the Trust would help with costs.

I hope they are keeping up the tradition. House staff can often feel very much alone in an unfeeling world. Call it paranoia, but there are moments when you feel that no one else – even colleagues at regional and head office – appreciates the day-to-day problems you are struggling with. It's wonderful to have a rare chance to talk with others who have real empathy with your situation. Occasionally you learn ways of dealing with *some* of the difficulties.

Another hat for the collection

In the years we had been at Felbrigg, I had been called in to help in most areas of the house – acting as room warden, selling tickets, recruiting, doing PR work, assisting visiting advisers, moving furniture and pictures, dealing with visitors' problems, cleaning chandeliers, clerking, washing and darning base camp chair-covers . . . I had also spent my share of time in the tearoom and kitchens, helping in the self-service bar, clearing tables, and washing up at times when the aged dish-washing machine decided it couldn't possibly manage another single spoon. I particularly remember one busy bank holiday when Joan called me to ask if I could do a stint loading and unloading the dish-washer as her staff were all too busy to attend to it and the dishes were piling high. At the time, the old machine was set very close to the ground and by the end of the afternoon, having spent hours bending with heavy trays of crockery, I thought my back would never straighten again.

'I know,' said Joan with feeling. 'This kitchen was obviously designed by a man. And *he* wasn't going to be working here.'

Her new kitchen, in the Park Restaurant, is much more convenient, I'm glad to say. She had a say in the design of that herself.

In December, with the Park Restaurant fully occupied doing Christmas lunches, Joan found herself short of an assistant to run the tearoom in the Old Kitchen, which provided self-service snacks. None of her usual deputies was available at the time, so, since I was well acquainted with the routines of the tearoom, she asked if I would step in just to keep the Old Kitchen going until we closed for Christmas. Many of our visitors, coming for

Christmas shopping, would want only a quick cup of coffee, or a sandwich, and with the Park fully occupied providing hot meals and special booked Christmas lunches it couldn't cope with snacks too.

Once I got into the swing of it all, I enjoyed being fully occupied in the tearoom, making sandwiches and setting out cakes and scones in the morning; cooking soup in the big urn, and heating pasties for lunchtime, all with assistance from one or other of Joan's ladies. If Chris and Eddie were going to be busy about the house, he would switch the phone through to us, so we could answer that, too, in case we weren't busy enough already. I wasn't sorry when he at last acquired a secretary who relieved me of telephonist duties – in the mornings, anyway.

All part of the service

One gloomy Sunday during my stint as tearoom manager, trouble brewed off-stage. It was one of those 'dark days before Christmas' when the dawn seems too weary to push aside the last vestiges of night and all day the world is wrapped in cloudy gloaming, only too willing to give way to a new night's first beckoning finger. Not many people came Christmas shopping on that day, and Lilian and I, in the tearoom, wondered if we were ever going to get rid of the big urn of soup we had made.

Over in the Park Restaurant the tale was different. Joan and her staff were bustling about serving a full house. Her special Christmas lunches, served on every Sunday in December, are always fully booked well in advance and that day was no exception. The early starters were well into their main course and the later people were beginning to arrive when, to Joan's horror, an extra party of six turned up. They were not down on the list, but the gentleman in charge of the party insisted he had booked a table, in the name of Smith.

'I phoned and made the reservation myself only yesterday,' he informed the embarrassed Joan in tones which threatened to reach the ears of other diners.

Such a mistake in our system seemed unlikely, but no one is infallible. 'I don't understand what can have happened,' Joan

Once I got into the swing of it all, I enjoyed
being fully occupied in the tearoom . . .

said. 'We've been fully booked for ages. I'm terribly sorry. Who did you speak to?'

'I didn't ask his name! I booked a table for six. For today, at one o'clock. He said that would be in order.'

'It was a man?'

'Certainly it was a man.' Mr Smith was not best pleased. He could see that the tables were rapidly filling as other parties who *were* on the list arrived and took their places. 'And he definitely promised us there would be a table available. What are you going to do about it?'

'If you wouldn't mind waiting a minute . . .' Joan hurried off to phone Chris and explain the situation. Had *he* taken the booking?

He had not – he had turned down several hopefuls because he knew the tables had all been booked for some time. The only other possibility was Eddie.

Joan told Chris that she would ask Mr Smith and his friends if they would mind waiting a while in the hope that a table might clear before too long, though from previous experience she knew that was unlikely. When people settle down to a Christmas lunch at Felbrigg they like to take their time and it is often four o'clock or after before they finally depart, which is why the entire restaurant is reserved solely for these special meals on December Sundays.

Chris went off to find Eddie, who was cleaning the glass lanterns in the Bird Corridor. His answer was just what Chris had expected: knowing that the restaurant was full, he had not taken any extra bookings, and certainly not yesterday. Since he and Chris were the only men around to answer the phone, the mystery remained.

While they were talking, Joan came over from the main restaurant in the stableyard to say that Mr Smith was becoming restive and ever more angry. Would Chris please come and speak to him?

Chris would. He was always available as a last resort to deal with tricky situations, wherever and whenever they might arise. It is his contention that anyone can make a mistake; how they deal with the consequences is what matters. In this case, since the mistake appeared to be ours – however mystifyingly – he and Joan agreed that the only thing to do would be to offer Mr Smith and party a free lunch, if they wouldn't mind taking it in the Old Kitchen.

On their way back to the stables and the Park Restaurant, they stopped off to warn Lilian and me of what was happening. We were to be ready with glasses of sherry as a first offering to smooth ruffled feathers.

Faced with the by-now fuming Mr Smith, Chris could only apologize for what must have been a break-down in our booking routine. Perhaps the party would care to lunch in the Old Kitchen . . . at Felbrigg's expense, of course. It was quieter there, anyway, the ambience perhaps even more conducive to a celebratory lunch, with rows of gleaming copper pans on the walls and the ghosts of many other Christmases swirling in the air.

'Well . . .' Mr Smith allowed himself to be somewhat mollified. 'As it happens I do prefer the Old Kitchen. So much more cosy. Very well. You did say a *free* lunch . . . ?'

So they trooped over to the Old Kitchen, through the newly renovated stable and the lobby of the new toilet block, down an alley between buildings, and across the spacious grass court-yard to the green door, all in the gloom of a dark December day. Lilian and I greeted them with smiles and complimentary sherry, showing them to the table we had hurriedly prepared in festive array. Fortunately, other visitors were still few, so Mr Smith and his party had the Old Kitchen tearoom almost to themselves, under that huge high ceiling where, of old, cooks and potboys had toiled amid steam and roasting fires.

While all preserved an outward show of insouciance, behind the scenes there was chaos and puzzlement. Joan returned to her duties in the Park, where her staff were busy looking after their full house. The rest of us switched gear to cope with Mr Smith.

In the tearoom we didn't have the proper plates and dishes, or the food promised on the special Christmas menu. Everything had to be brought over from the Park Restaurant. While Lilian and I switched on warming ovens and cleared spaces, and looked after both the Smith party and other customers who came in for snacks, Chris rushed to and fro, first bringing a great pan of soup, with dishes in which to serve it.

This journeying between Park Restaurant and Old Kitchen was a bit like doing several circuits of the Grand National course. The new restaurant kitchens are at the far end of the stable block, and the restaurant windows overlook the stable-yard; anyone coming to or going from the kitchen by the quickest route from the Hall would, on that day, be in full view of dozens of merry lunchers. By now they were well into their meal and their wine, wearing paper hats and pulling crackers, the noise of laughter and conversation spilling out with the electric light to enliven the afternoon dusk. Chris didn't want to raise speculation by appearing, like a manic spectre at the feast, rushing backward and forward across the stableyard with trays of comestibles. He went by the back way, his route lying through tenants' gardens, round shrubs and hedges, between bushes, and over flowerbeds and little fences, via wicket gates and narrow stone steps to a final latched gateway under an arch and into the grass courtyard. Branches caught at his clothes and hair, the steps were slippery with damp and lichen, the trays were shiny, the plates kept sliding . . .

While Lilian and I served the soup, Chris made several journeys to bring plates of turkey, chipolatas, roast and purée potatoes, Brussels sprouts, *petits pois*, stuffings, sauces, and gravy. All went into the warming ovens along with the big dinner plates which he also brought. Joan dashed over briefly to help serve up the main course – to make sure it was presented to her own high standards – then went back to oversee her crowded, convivial restaurant.

And all the time, we were racking our brains wondering how this mix-up could have happened. Mr Smith was adamant that a man had answered the phone and assured him that a table was available. Yet apart from Chris and Eddie there was no man who could have taken such a call. Had it, perhaps, been a woman with a deep voice? Perhaps someone had got the wrong date? Or turned over two pages in the diary? But none of the answers we came up with was entirely satisfactory.

Somewhere between the main course and the pudding, when the Smith party was steadily munching at generous helpings of turkey and Chris was catching his breath after making an extra journey to fetch more cream (he had spilt the first lot during a fifth circuit of the steeplechase course), he had a sudden brainwave. It led him to telephone the restaurant at Blickling Hall.

'How are you getting on with your Christmas lunches?' he asked Stewart, the Blickling catering manager. 'Did all your parties arrive? You're not, by chance, waiting for a party of six?'

'You must be clairvoyant!' came the reply. 'Yes, we've been waiting since one o'clock for them to turn up. Party in the name of Smith. He phoned yesterday. I took the booking myself.'

Ah . . .

It's an easy enough mistake to make. If you look in the phone book under 'National Trust', our number and Blickling's are right next to each other. A slip of the eye, or the finger, and anyone could get it wrong.

Mr Smith and his friends were tucking into their Christmas pudding and cream when Chris appeared beside their table, all mine-host amiability, hoping that they were enjoying their meal. They were. The sherry, the good food and the warm atmosphere had done a lot to abate their annoyance.

'By the way,' Chris added, 'we think we've solved the mystery over the booking.'

'Oh, really?' The celebrants were agog to hear the answer.

'Did you look the number up in the phone book?' Chris asked Mr Smith.

'Why . . . yes.'

'Do you think it's possible you dialled the wrong one? You see, they're waiting for a party of six, in the name of Smith, over at Blickling.'

Poor Mr Smith was mortified. 'Oh dear me. Yes. Yes, I could easily have . . . Oh dear. What a stupid mistake. I think we'd better pay for our lunch, after all.'

Joan was relieved that an unpleasant incident had been

resolved amicably, with an extra six Christmas lunches sold. In fact, we were all pleased that Felbrigg had coped with the emergency – even if we *were* left with a totally exhausted administrator!

More Christmas cheer

The approach of Christmas brings its usual crop of parties. We host an annual lunch for the tenant farmers and their wives, an occasion attended by the land agent, the administrator, the houseman, and their wives. In my experience it was always a delight to meet the farmers with whom we were in only tenuous contact throughout the rest of the year.

Mid-month we held our staff party, though it became increasingly difficult to cram everyone in when numbers rose beyond a hundred. For supper we filled not only the Old Kitchen but the Bird Corridor, too, and getting everyone into the Morning Room to listen to the usual speeches of thanks was an impossibility – some were always left out in the lobby. 'I always liked playing Sardines,' our dear friend Harry, the joker, laughed. Still, it was the one annual chance to get everybody together, to make them all feel they were part of the Felbrigg team, whether outdoor or indoor staff, from the youngest waitress, in her teens, to the oldest room warden, in his eighties.

Since we had that huge sitting room in our flat, we also used it for private parties of our own, such as a gathering of the local writers' group to which I belonged. No one ever refused an invitation to come to Felbrigg.

A unique event

Often in December Felbrigg holds a Christmas concert with a special Christmas programme, but in our final few weeks at the house Chris decided to change the pattern and, rather than a concert, offer a talk on some of the secrets of the house, to be followed by a candlelit supper. He decided to make it a black tie event, a really special occasion when we might all have a chance to dress up and relive some of the glamour of former times. By then many local people were aware that he was an excellent, entertaining and informative speaker. The tickets were soon sold, most of them to regular concert-goers.

It was marvellous welcoming our elegant guests as they arrived that dark night. We had lit the Hall to look its best with light blazing from every window, our vast Christmas tree sparkling from the sitting room above, and ourselves decked in our best evening wear. The Morning Room was arranged with chairs in front of a long table on which Chris had set out mysterious containers and cardboard boxes, with more hidden behind the long baize cloth that covered the table. One could feel the buzz of curiosity and anticipation as the room filled.

Once more he brought out those seldom-seen treasures which never failed to elicit surprise and wonder in whatever audience he was addressing. For instance, those antique chocolate boxes, made of cardboard and trimmed with velvet, gilt lace and ribbons, in the shape of a harp and a violin complete with strings – their survival is a miracle. There are books with Samuel Johnson's handwritten notes in the margin; rediscovered watercolours of the Norwich school; an ostrich egg etched with a scene of a sailing ship; a mourning ring inlaid with jet and inscribed for Susan Kitton – the family name was changed after they became squires of Felbrigg, Ketton being considered more euphonious. So many fascinating things, large and small, valuable or not, most of them irreplaceable.

I've already mentioned a few of the treasures Chris would show on such occasions, but, though it is hard to choose from such a plenitude, one of the most interesting items is the set of filigree jewellery, bracelets and necklace, made of iron. It comes from Prussia, dating from the time of the Napoleonic Wars. In order to fund the war effort, the Emperor asked the ladies of his court to donate their jewels to the cause. In return he gave them substitute jewellery, of delicate filigree wrought from the iron of a captured French cannon. One can easily imagine the pride with which those ladies must have worn their unusual decorations, as a sign that they had given their gold and diamonds to aid their country. The jewellery feels strange in the hand, heavier than it looks, but extraordinarily delicate considering its material. How it came to Felbrigg is another of those unanswered questions.

Every time he gave such a talk, Chris's enthusiasm shone through to make what he was saying all the more absorbing – even to me, and I had heard it a dozen times or more. It was even more moving on this occasion – knowing it would be the last time that he, and I, would enjoy this privilege.

Christmases past

In a previous year, late in December, there had been an evening when children from the local Sunday school sang carols beneath our window and we leaned out to listen to them before taking our lanterns and joining them in the grass courtyard to serenade the tenants. Afterwards we all repaired to The Retreat for hot mince pies and coffee. My mother came to spend that earlier Christmas with us and joined us for a final drink in the Park Restaurant before everyone went off for the holiday. For a few days, Felbrigg would be completely closed.

But quiet? Hardly.

Since it was our turn to be on duty, and since we knew that some of our staff and volunteers were going to be alone for the holiday, we had sent out a general invitation for people to come for drinks on Christmas morning in the hour or so between church and lunch. With a rush of blood to the head, Chris had added a word to the effect that any family and/or guests who happened to be staying would be welcome, too.

For a long time now, we have made it a habit to eat our Christmas dinner in the evening, which means we can relax for the early part of the day. There is no scramble to get up early to put the turkey in the oven and we don't spend the afternoon dozing in an overstuffed stupor. We generally have a light lunch and all help to prepare the dinner in easy stages.

That Christmas began with a bright, crisp morning and, as we warmed up the big icy sitting room and set out bowls of nuts and nibbles in preparation, we did wonder if anyone would bother to come. What we had forgotten was the magnetism of Felbrigg. No one ever refused an invitation to visit us there.

Once the doorbell started ringing Chris was kept busy, up and down the stairs, as a steady stream of visitors arrived. Before long, *sixty* people were crammed into our sitting room, much to my poor mother's bemusement – staff, volunteers, and their friends and families.

Luckily we had bought a case of wine not long before, we had plenty of crisps and nuts, and our sitting room was enormous, so what else mattered? Body heat helped to warm the room as conversation and laughter filled the space under the high ceiling, and beyond the huge bay windows the park lay peaceful in winter sunlight, grazed by unheeding cows. Our guests leaned on the windowboards and sighed over the view.

'Goodness, aren't you lucky!' someone exclaimed.

On such occasions, surrounded by friends – yes, we were.

On the third day of Christmas . . .

Boxing Day that year passed quietly, which was probably just as well because on the 27th Felbrigg was due to welcome four coachloads of out-of-season visitors.

Anticipating this extra open day, we had put out a list asking for volunteer room wardens, not expecting many offers at that season. But yet again we had been amazed by the willingness of Felbrigg's friends to step in and help out. The list was filled without trouble, and on the due day the ladies and gentlemen turned up, delighted to be part of this unusual session. It made a change on those often dead days between Christmas and New Year, and the volunteers were interested to see the Hall in its new case covers, all ready for winter – it's not often that they have the chance to see familiar rooms in this guise.

Our visitors that day were staying at the Hotel Nelson in Norwich over the holiday. A visit to Felbrigg was part of their Christmas package, arranged in earlier consultation with Chris, of course. They were coming to see the Hall in winter drapes and to have sherry and mince pies in the Old Kitchen, some in the morning and some in the afternoon.

Just before the first two coaches were expected to arrive, a Range Rover drew up outside, pulling a trailer. When Chris went out to see what was happening, he discovered that the driver and his companions were hoping to launch a hot air balloon. Did we mind if they did it from our front grass? Chris agreed, having ascertained that the wind was blowing away from the Hall, and the men began to unpack their trailer and inflate their red and white balloon.

In the midst of all this, the coaches from the Hotel Nelson appeared and drew into the front courtyard, passengers all staring in surprise at the spectacle, which they thought had been arranged for their benefit. The balloon *did* add an exotic touch to the day. When fully expanded it lifted slowly off and drifted away from the Hall – heading straight for a bank of trees. Everyone watched in growing alarm as the basket rose sluggishly under its colourful balloon, the burners shooting out orange flames. Slowly, slowly . . . the basket *just* managed to scrape over the trees.

Somehow, that exciting start to their visit gave our guests the idea that it was 'anything goes' at Felbrigg at Christmas. They went wandering in all kinds of strange directions and had to be shepherded back. I even found a couple of ladies climbing the stairs to our flat: 'Up here, dear. This looks like the shop.' Well, I did keep my collection of small plates on the shelves at the first half-landing, so perhaps the mistake was understandable!

In the afternoon we repeated the exercise – but without the balloon.

After that interlude, business continued as usual when, the following day, Heather and her helpers were in checking the shop stock. Soon the year was ending with a big family dinner, Andy with his girlfriend, Kevin with his wife, several friends – a party of twelve in all. Another year loomed in prospect. Work went on.

Cobwebs

In 1990, the approach of the publication of *Cobwebs and Cream Teas* attracted a good deal of publicity, mostly because Felbrigg itself made such a good subject. The media started to call – magazines, newspapers, radio and television; they were interested in talking to both of us, for, though I had written the book, Chris was of necessity the star of it.

Among other things, *Woman's Weekly* printed a colour feature on 'The Tenants of Felbrigg Hall', and later the *Daily Telegraph* printed an interview, with a large picture. Chris and I were on Radio Five with Johnny Walker, and on Radio Norfolk and Radio Broadland, not to mention an hour on our local hospital radio. The book was reviewed in many places, including *The Times* (Heavens! What fame). We also made two live TV broadcasts, one from Pebble Mill in Birmingham on their lunchtime show, with Judy Spiers, and one at Sky TV, from their studio in London, with Tony Blackburn and Jenny Hanley.

In the middle of all this excitement, with Eddie away on a well-earned holiday, Chris rose early one Tuesday morning to open up the house and had reached the Library when he was assailed by a wave of nausea accompanied by a sudden vertigo which felled him. Somehow he managed to crawl back to the flat and into bed and I sent for the doctor. Meanwhile, being the only person there to do it, I finished unlocking the house and let in the cleaners, the book conservators, and a carpenter.

The doctor diagnosed labyrinthitis, a disease of the inner ear which makes the sufferer unable to keep his balance. It could last anything from a day or two to a couple of weeks and Chris had to stay in bed this time – if he tried to get up, he fell over.

Having been told to let regional office know at once if this kind of emergency arose again, I tried to contact our land agent, but he was out for the day and his secretary didn't know who else to consult for help; so I held the fort. It was mid-evening before Simon finally phoned and said he had arranged with George Blake to stand in for a day or two, until we saw how long Chris's labyrinthitis would last.

Friday of that week was our appointed day to go to London to appear live on Sky TV's morning magazine programme. Chris hoped to be able to go, and to test his fitness he dragged himself out of bed on Thursday afternoon to give his promised chat to the guides at one of their early-year 'Guides Talks'. He managed it, though he went straight back to bed afterwards, insisting that if he rested he would be fit enough to go with me to London.

We were travelling by train, so we had planned to be up at 5.30 a.m. to drive to Cromer for a local service that would connect us with the Inter-City express at Norwich.

With my reluctance to crawl out of bed in the mornings, 5.30 a.m. was penance enough, but in the event we were up at four: the alarms went off yet again. By the time we had established that this was another fault and not a fire, it was hardly worth going back to bed so we got ready and set out for the station. Stoically battling through moments of lingering nausea and vertigo, Chris somehow managed the train journey and to save him the hassle of the underground we took a taxi to St John's Wood.

The Sky TV people could not have been kinder. Tony Blackburn and Jenny Hanley were a delight to talk to, the interview produced a lot of laughter, and we even got to sit on the couch with Dr Mike Smith, from the Jimmy Young radio programme. We were on air for nearly half an hour – terrific exposure for the book. However, Chris was not feeling too well and as soon as he got the chance he went out into the street for a breath of air. It was only when people started giving him strange looks that he realized he was still wearing his thick television makeup!

Back to earth

That weekend Eddie was back and we were due to take a few days' break, so I hoped Chris would relax and get over his labyrinthitis. We were both on a high after our trip to London, but since Chris felt shattered we decided not to go far and on Saturday he stayed in bed until eleven. Then Joan arrived at the flat door anxious about arrangements for a special lunch party which was to take place in the Park Restaurant. A family was celebrating their grandfather's ninetieth birthday, which was fine, all arranged long ago, but now they had phoned to say that someone had composed a special piece of music and wished to play it to the old gentleman with the twenty-odd guests present. Could they possibly use the Morning Room piano?

Chris agreed that they could, if Eddie didn't mind organizing it all; so Joan, Eddie and I spent half an hour rearranging the

Morning Room for the event. By the time we finished, a still wobbly Chris was up and dressed and we decided to go and have coffee and a quiet lunch in the Park Restaurant. Well, that was the plan.

It was a cold, windy winter day. Guests for the birthday lunch began to arrive three-quarters of an hour early and we saw Eddie directing them into the main Hall, out of the weather. As the arrangements had been changed, he had to be outside to tell them to gather in the Morning Room rather than in the restaurant, but that meant the Morning Room and the lobbies were unstewarded, and we could see some small children among the groups. Help! Although we were in the middle of lunch, Chris left me and, worried for the safety of his Hall, went off to supervise affairs inside the house.

With a large table reserved for the party, the other tables soon filled up – even on winter Saturdays, Felbrigg was a popular meeting place for lunch – so when it became obvious that our table was needed I took my coffee into the kitchen. There, I discovered that one of the waitresses had gone off sick and the washing-up was piling high, so I spent the next couple of hours loading and unloading the dish-washer. When Chris eventually returned he joined me at the task despite my pleas to him to go back to the flat. 'I couldn't rest,' he said. 'I'm all right, I've got my adrenaline going.'

So had I! Yesterday I'd been a star, today it was back to reality. Good for the soul, I suppose.

As the year progressed and the book appeared in the shops I lost count of the number of times I was called down to sign copies. Many people arrived at the ticket desk saying they had come because they had read the book and wanted to see the place for themselves, which was lovely to hear. Felbrigg is worth seeing.

Radio interlude

The funniest episode with the media was when we went to Norwich, to Radio Norfolk, for a link-up with *The Ken Bruce Show*, which at that time was broadcast for two hours in the evening. The interview was to go on air around twenty past ten, though it was recorded a little earlier to allow for retakes if necessary. At that time of night, only a skeleton staff was on duty at Radio Norfolk. We were met by a lady who said she had often done this sort of thing before, though never at night when no support staff were there. Still, she couldn't see why anything should go wrong.

People really should beware of making such remarks! When we got into the studio, she couldn't make the link with London. She flipped switches, flicked microphones, called soulfully into the void. Everything was dead. She didn't know what had gone wrong. Maybe something was unplugged. The three of us ended up crawling on the floor, under desks and behind equipment, looking for disconnected leads and not finding any. All the time, the clock was ticking away towards the time when we should be recording.

In desperation the lady decided to go and see if there was a duty engineer somewhere, leaving Chris and me sitting in the silent studio. It felt eerie. We couldn't go anywhere – it was all locked up. In fact, when I had asked if there was a toilet the lady had had to escort me, punching in security numbers to unlock every door on the way.

At last she returned. Panic over. She had found an engineer and he had investigated and discovered that a switch had not been set back to normal after a link-up with Yarmouth earlier. Phew! Just in time. Broadcasting House came on the line, checked sound levels, and suddenly I was talking to Ken Bruce.

'We'll start at the end of this piece of music,' he told me, and we listened as a record played itself out. 'Here in the studio with me,' he lied to the listening millions, 'I have Mary Mackie . . .'

The ten-minute interview lasted about ten seconds, so it seemed. Soon we were being let out through all those locked doors again, into the lamplit streets of Norwich, to make the journey back to the coast. We heard the interview over the car radio.

When we got in, I phoned my mother to ask if she had heard the broadcast, too. She had, of course. 'But, where are you calling from?' she asked.

'From Felbrigg.'

'What? How on earth did you get home so fast? He said you were in the studio with him.'

Ah, the miracles of modern technology.

7

～⌒～⌒～

Back in the real world . . .

The early year brought a sudden sense of time running out. The end of March, and the beginning of the new season, loomed ever larger. The diary was filled with meetings to be held, people to be seen, jobs to be done.

The Hamilton Kerr Institute sent experts to take down some of our paintings for restoration, and soon afterwards men came to replace on the Drawing Room wall a picture of the Battle of the Texel: Mr Ketton-Cremer had sold it to the National Maritime Museum and it now came back on permanent loan, to rejoin its partner flanking the Drawing Room door. The museum had glazed the picture and insisted it remained glazed, which made it extra heavy and difficult to see clearly with the light across it. Its partner remains unglazed. If you go to Felbrigg, see which you prefer.

The cleaners were busy, working on the last few bedrooms, sweeping, dusting, polishing, mending . . .

Still, even in the most frantic weeks there are moments for relaxation. One year Joan and I snatched a day off and went to a catering exhibition in Yarmouth. Another year, Chris and I took a couple of days away to attend Kevin's Passing Out Parade at RAF Cranwell, from which he emerged as a Flying Officer in Princess Mary's Royal Air Force Nursing Service. Another proud day for us personally.

Icing on the cake

Snow ... When it falls at Felbrigg it lays a magic blanket on winter-weary woods and gardens. The park outside glistens under the sun, the trees become puffs of pure white candyfloss on dark trunks and every branch and twig is emphasized by a line of light.

For two or three years running in the late 1980s, snow fell thick and soft in the weeks after Christmas, cutting us off from the rest of the world and wrapping us in a white shawl, whose light penetrated all our rooms. No workmen could reach us, nor our cleaners. For once the Hall really was quiet. Venturing out into the gardens, we made the first human footprints on that undulating whiteness, though we could see where birds and cats had been – and a fox. The donkeys came from their shed to say hello, greedily snatching at handfuls of grass that we excavated from its frozen duvet. Out in the open park the wind had swirled the snow into wonderful shapes and mounds, all crusted on top so that you could walk on them, with care – and if you did fall through it was no harm done.

Along by the walled garden, a great frozen wave of snow hung for days as if waiting for some bold surfer to come and ride its crest, and all the contours of the countryside were changed. One day Chris was talking with the gardeners and one of the tenants in the stableyard when he stumbled and fell backwards into a four-foot drift. He couldn't get purchase to pull himself out; every time he tried, the snow crust gave way. Ted and Mark stood by helpless with laughter while Dick rushed off to get his camera and record the event before the struggling Chris was helped to his feet.

One year, the drive was completely impassable in both directions. We were snowed in for two weeks, except that the men could get out by tractor through the woods; they kept us supplied with milk from the nearest small shop on the main road. But other food ran low and as our freezer emptied I phoned Joan and asked if I could dip into her restaurant supplies of frozen vegetables, on the understanding that we would replace whatever we used.

That was the situation when Kevin phoned to say that he and Alison planned to come over for a couple of days, by train since the roads were blocked. We told them we were snowed in but they were not deterred; they would come by rail to Cromer, get a taxi as far as they could, and trek the rest on foot. They were eager to see what Felbrigg was like when snowbound.

'We shall be glad to see you,' we said. 'Will you please bring us some bread and meat? Anything will do.'

Preparing for their arrival, I baked a pie with the last meat out of our own freezer — twelve pigeon breasts, donated to us by Barney, one of our room-warden friends who had a share in a shoot.

Knowing what time the train was due, we walked out to meet Kevin and Alison and encountered them at the far end of the snowed-up driveway. They had managed to get from Cromer and part way down the drive by taxi, as far as the Home Farm turning. From there, the road up the rise and through the car-park was still deep in drifted snow, impossible for traffic. We were glad to see our young pair fording through the drifts as the light failed, and almost equally glad of the provisions they brought with them — lamb chops, minced beef, and two large loaves of bread.

We dined on the tasty pie I had made, though we didn't tell them what meat it contained until they had finished it and declared their enjoyment of it. Then we asked them what they thought the meat was. Steak and kidney, they guessed. No. Liver, then? We could see them getting more and more worried as all the more palatable possibilities made us shake our heads. Eventually, we had to confess it was pigeon.

Ugh! They both agreed they wouldn't have eaten it if they'd known.

That evening, at about eight o'clock, Chris answered the phone and found himself speaking to Simon, the land agent. The three of us, listening to Chris's end of the conversation, deduced that someone wanted to come and visit us the next day. Someone important, evidently.

'You know we're still snowed up?' Chris said. 'I could try to get someone to open the drive, I suppose. Or, if not, he could always come in via the farm and round the back way. I'll have a word with the farmer. Do you think he'll want lunch?'

While the conversation went on, Kevin, Alison and I sat looking at each other, silently speculating on the identity of this prospective visitor.

'Who is it?' we asked when eventually Chris put down the phone. 'Some Trust bigwig?'

'Oh, no, nobody like that. Actually ... it's the Prince of Wales.'

'Ha ha, Dad,' said Kevin, used to his father's drolleries.

But this time it wasn't a joke.

We were about to have a visit from Prince Charles. He was staying at Sandringham and, the shooting being curtailed by the snow, had expressed a wish to see some National Trust properties, including Felbrigg. Well ... perhaps. Nothing was definite. They would let us know for sure by ten o'clock next morning.

'And *will* he want lunch?' I asked, thinking of my empty store cupboards.

'Yes, he might do. Better get something ready in case. Nothing grand. Just a snack will do.'

What? 'For how many?'

'Simon wasn't sure. But it won't be too many. It's a private visit, not an official one. And we're not to tell anyone. They don't want a lot of photographers and spectators snooping around.'

Only Chris and I were to meet the prince and then Chris would show him round the Hall. On this highly informal occasion, the visitor was not to be addressed as 'Your Royal Highness', even on first greeting: 'Sir' would do, if any appellation at all was necessary.

I hardly slept for worrying about the possibility of having to feed the prince and his entourage on what little we had. I was up early (which in itself says a lot for my state of mind), cleaning up the flat. Kev and Alison pitched in to help. You have never seen a place so swiftly and thoroughly spring-cleaned. Lord, why hadn't I washed my windows? I'd been meaning to do it for weeks!

Chris got on the phone, alerting the Home Farm not to worry if they saw cars sweeping up their drive and through their yards to reach us by a farm track which the comings and goings of cows and tractors had opened up. He didn't say who was coming, though he fancied the farmer had guessed it might be royalty. Nor did he tell Bullens when he phoned to ask if one of their men could possibly get hold of a snowplough and clear the drive. They said they would send someone with a board on the front of a JCB. 'Be there as soon as we can.' Good old Bullens, always reliable in an emergency.

That done, Chris went round the Hall opening the shutters, switching on heaters and getting out a few things he thought might interest the prince, such as a family tree which shows a tenuous connection between the Windhams and the Spencers of Althorp, and a book of eighteenth-century maps enclosed in a soft leather binding, designed to be rolled up and stuffed in a greatcoat pocket. William Cobbett may have used such a book of maps on his 'rural rides'. The Hall was, of course, shrouded in its winter dust covers, and dark on that chill, misty day, so Chris plugged in the lamps and switched them on in readiness all through the house.

I made some broth with the meat Kevin had brought – it was *disgusting* stuff, the most awful soup I had ever made. I prayed that His Royal Highness wouldn't need to eat any of it. If he came at all. The time went on. Maybe he wasn't coming. All that panic for nothing.

Simon had said he would hear definite news by ten o'clock. When ten o'clock came and went, we assumed something had happened to change the prince's plans. What a shame! Or was it a relief? Chris phoned regional office to confirm whether the visit had been called off. He asked to speak to Simon, but Simon wasn't there and his secretary, who, like everyone else, had been sworn to secrecy, was not about to divulge *anything*.

'Look, I already *know* what's supposed to be happening,' Chris said at last. 'Just tell me – can we expect a very important visitor to arrive at Felbrigg or not?'

'Well . . . yes,' the secretary reluctantly admitted. 'He'll be there after lunch.'

After lunch. Thank heaven for that! Now only the family would be forced to sup my awful soup.

It was hard keeping the news to ourselves. We wanted to ring round the tenants so they might see the visitor, too, but having been warned not to we desisted. We did, however, think that His Royal Highness wouldn't mind too much if Kevin and Alison just stood by to lock the door behind us, watch out for any callers, and man the phones.

After lunch, we saw Bullens' JCB come toiling through the car-park; Chris went out and asked the driver to keep out of the way if he saw cars coming. He had just cleared the way right up to the front courtyard when through the freezing mist we saw lights approaching. Three vehicles. A Range Rover with Prince Charles at the wheel and a lady beside him who proved to be Lady Susan Hussey, wife of the chairman of the BBC and one of the Queen's ladies-in-waiting; behind them came a detective in a Land Rover, and behind him a final car containing Simon and another member of regional office staff.

Chris and I waited by the main door while Kevin and Alison stood well off to one side, not to intrude. The prince strode up, smiling and relaxed as he shook hands with us, then went without hesitation to greet the startled Kevin and Alison and ask who they were and what they were doing there.

Then it was into the Hall. 'Shall I take my boots off?' His Royal Highness enquired, but Chris didn't think it was necessary as the prince's blue moonboots were quite clean and dry once he had wiped them on the mat. (Blue moonboots, not green wellies; and instead of a waxed green jacket a navy one marked 'Supertramp' – after the pop group, in case anyone's wondering.) From then on, whenever any summer visitor balked at being asked to remove unsuitable footwear, such as stiletto heels, we had an impeccable precedent to quote 'Even the Prince of Wales was willing to walk round in his socks.'

He went ahead with Chris while I tagged along behind chatting with Lady Susan and the detective. The prince was so friendly that we were all relaxed; it was like showing old friends round the Hall. He was interested in everything Chris showed him, and helped to lift the dust covers to look at the wonderful red and brass gleam of our boulle furniture, and the tall gilt torchères. He was amazed by the length of some icicles visible

'Shall I take my boots off?' His Royal Highness enquired.

at the rear of the house, hanging forty-odd feet from the gutters beside the attics, and intrigued by the sanitary arrangements of the former squires.

He confided to Chris that he had not realized that National Trust houses were fully furnished – he had been under the impression they were empty, much like French *châteaux*. For over an hour we were privileged to enjoy his company and share our delight in Felbrigg.

At the end of the visit, Prince Charles strode soft-footed into the Morning Room where Alison was looking out of the window, and startled her afresh by making some casual remark when she hadn't realized he was there. Kevin was outside. I hope the prince didn't guess that our son had been peeking in the royal Range Rover and was delighted to see that on the floor lay a pair of spare shoes: 'Brown brogues. Just like mine!'

As the three vehicles moved away, merging with the mist, their red tail lights blinking out pair by pair, we stood watching in silence, mesmerized by disbelief. It was a day or two before we could believe it had really happened.

Of all our memories of Felbrigg, this remains one of the proudest: we have met the Prince of Wales, in total informality, without crowds of onlookers, hangers-on and pervasive press. Sadly, we have no photographs – to produce a camera on such an occasion would, as the Princess Royal might have observed, have been decidedly naff. But we shall never forget that we had the good fortune to be at Felbrigg just when His Royal Highness was considering becoming Patron of the National Trust's Coast and Countryside Appeal, a post he assumed soon afterwards.

So the snows melt. In the Orangery the camellias are in bud, bursting again into glorious waxen flower. The Old Vicarage at Holt advertises its annual Primrose Days, and soon the daffodils will be out once again across the apron of grass that fronts Felbrigg Hall. Another season begins.

Completing the set

The one area in which I had not worked during our time at Felbrigg was the shop, but shortly before we left I achieved my ambition of adding that to my tally when one of the assistants was ill and Heather had to go off for a few minutes, leaving one of her rooms untended. She called me and asked would I mind . . . In the half-hour I was there I made a handsome profit – I sold a pencil and rubber to a small boy.

Eddie's wife Katie worked full-time in the shop with Heather and at busy times they had a lady named Pam as an extra helper. Pam and her husband John had been associated with Felbrigg from soon after it opened, both of them acting as room guides and with Pam also working in the shop. Over the years, along with so many of our Felbrigg acquaintances, they had become great personal friends.

Though no longer in the first flush of youth, Pam had enough energy and enthusiasm to put many a younger person to shame. But in our final year she confessed to me that, when she filled in her application form for part-time work, she had feared her real birthdate of 1911 might make her seem incredibly ancient. 'So I lied about it,' she admitted. 'Do you think they will mind if they find out?'

I was intrigued. How many years had she lopped off her real age? Ten? Twenty? 'What year did you put?' I asked.

'1914,' said she.

Endnote

Having Felbrigg Hall as our address was, all in all, an experience we would not have missed. We enjoyed sharing its delights with the many thousands of visitors who came every year. Well . . . most of them. However, we never forgot that we were temporary custodians, there to preserve and protect the Hall and its environs for the sake of the nation. That privilege, and pain, we have now passed on to others.

How could we bear to leave, you may wonder.

The answer to that is manifold. Some of the reasons were

personal; some had to do with the hourly annoyances and frustrations that you may have detected between the lines of this book. Still, there were marvellous things about our life at Felbrigg, and we made many good friends with whom we keep in touch. We would not have missed the experience for worlds.

And perhaps it was time to leave, anyway. Chris cared too much about the place, risking his health in his efforts to do a good job for the National Trust, for Felbrigg itself and, not least, for the staff and volunteers who were his responsibility. I believe he succeeded. He put Felbrigg squarely on the map and left a lovely team spirit abiding there. We trust that its new custodians, and those that follow them, will love it and care for it as much as we did.

But, with us or without us, the story goes on. The seasons turn through the excitement of opening in the spring, through a crowded summer, a quieter autumn and a hectic winter with all its cleaning and conservation work. We are no longer there to share in it but Felbrigg will go on, I hope, for your delight, and for your children, and their children, providing a brief escape from bad news, from wars and politics and all the other stresses of modern life. Do go and see it, if you can, and give it my love.

Next time you're visiting a stately home and marvelling at the treasures it contains, its furniture and pictures, its human stories both touching and tragic, its glorious architecture and its lovely setting, give a thought to what *still* goes on behind those baize doors. Not so much the romance of *Upstairs, Downstairs* as 'all hands to the pumps', be it death watch beetle, blocked loos, defrosted freezers, locked cars, lost children, stolen plants and lavatory chains, or intruder incidents at dead of night.

As one stately-home owner put it, 'In this business it's a case of being up to your elbow in a blocked drain one minute, and shaking hands with royalty the next.'

You just hope there's time to wash your hands in between!

If you do visit Felbrigg, you will find changes wrought since our time. Inevitably so. Eddie and Katie have moved on, too; the Old Kitchen is no longer a tearoom; the shop can now be found in the stable block; the Park Restaurant has altered its opening hours and new areas have been opened to public view. To find out about opening times, please consult The National Trust Handbook, *published annually, or pick up one of the many leaflets which you will find in tourist offices and other outlets.*